Letters written in France, in the Summer 1790, to a friend in England; containing, various anecdotes relative to the French revolution; and memoirs of Mons. and Madame du F----.

Helen Maria Williams

ECCO

PRINT EDITIONS

Letters written in France, in the Summer 1790, to a friend in England; containing, various anecdotes relative to the French revolution; and memoirs of Mons. and Madame du F----.
Williams, Helen Maria
ESTCID: T094829
Reproduction from British Library
Mons. du F----. = Augustin François Thomas du Fossé (Tourneux, Bibl. de l'hist. de Paris pendant la rév. française 1, p.67). With a half-title.
Text and register are continuous.
Dublin : printed for G. Burnet, P. Wogan, P. Byrne J. Moore, J. Jones, A. Grueber, W. Jones, R. White, and J. Rice, 1791.
[4],216,216-223p. ; 12°

Eighteenth Century
Collections Online
Print Editions

Gale ECCO Print Editions

Relive history with *Eighteenth Century Collections Online*, now available in print for the independent historian and collector. This series includes the most significant English-language and foreign-language works printed in Great Britain during the eighteenth century, and is organized in seven different subject areas including literature and language; medicine, science, and technology; and religion and philosophy. The collection also includes thousands of important works from the Americas.

The eighteenth century has been called "The Age of Enlightenment." It was a period of rapid advance in print culture and publishing, in world exploration, and in the rapid growth of science and technology – all of which had a profound impact on the political and cultural landscape. At the end of the century the American Revolution, French Revolution and Industrial Revolution, perhaps three of the most significant events in modern history, set in motion developments that eventually dominated world political, economic, and social life.

In a groundbreaking effort, Gale initiated a revolution of its own: digitization of epic proportions to preserve these invaluable works in the largest online archive of its kind. Contributions from major world libraries constitute over 175,000 original printed works. Scanned images of the actual pages, rather than transcriptions, recreate the works *as they first appeared.*

Now for the first time, these high-quality digital scans of original works are available via print-on-demand, making them readily accessible to libraries, students, independent scholars, and readers of all ages.

For our initial release we have created seven robust collections to form one the world's most comprehensive catalogs of 18th century works.

Initial Gale ECCO Print Editions collections include:

History and Geography
Rich in titles on English life and social history, this collection spans the world as it was known to eighteenth-century historians and explorers. Titles include a wealth of travel accounts and diaries, histories of nations from throughout the world, and maps and charts of a world that was still being discovered. Students of the War of American Independence will find fascinating accounts from the British side of conflict.

Social Science

Delve into what it was like to live during the eighteenth century by reading the first-hand accounts of everyday people, including city dwellers and farmers, businessmen and bankers, artisans and merchants, artists and their patrons, politicians and their constituents. Original texts make the American, French, and Industrial revolutions vividly contemporary.

Medicine, Science and Technology

Medical theory and practice of the 1700s developed rapidly, as is evidenced by the extensive collection, which includes descriptions of diseases, their conditions, and treatments. Books on science and technology, agriculture, military technology, natural philosophy, even cookbooks, are all contained here.

Literature and Language

Western literary study flows out of eighteenth-century works by Alexander Pope, Daniel Defoe, Henry Fielding, Frances Burney, Denis Diderot, Johann Gottfried Herder, Johann Wolfgang von Goethe, and others. Experience the birth of the modern novel, or compare the development of language using dictionaries and grammar discourses.

Religion and Philosophy

The Age of Enlightenment profoundly enriched religious and philosophical understanding and continues to influence present-day thinking. Works collected here include masterpieces by David Hume, Immanuel Kant, and Jean-Jacques Rousseau, as well as religious sermons and moral debates on the issues of the day, such as the slave trade. The Age of Reason saw conflict between Protestantism and Catholicism transformed into one between faith and logic -- a debate that continues in the twenty-first century.

Law and Reference

This collection reveals the history of English common law and Empire law in a vastly changing world of British expansion. Dominating the legal field is the *Commentaries of the Law of England* by Sir William Blackstone, which first appeared in 1765. Reference works such as almanacs and catalogues continue to educate us by revealing the day-to-day workings of society.

Fine Arts

The eighteenth-century fascination with Greek and Roman antiquity followed the systematic excavation of the ruins at Pompeii and Herculaneum in southern Italy; and after 1750 a neoclassical style dominated all artistic fields. The titles here trace developments in mostly English-language works on painting, sculpture, architecture, music, theater, and other disciplines. Instructional works on musical instruments, catalogs of art objects, comic operas, and more are also included.

The BiblioLife Network

This project was made possible in part by the BiblioLife Network (BLN), a project aimed at addressing some of the huge challenges facing book preservationists around the world. The BLN includes libraries, library networks, archives, subject matter experts, online communities and library service providers. We believe every book ever published should be available as a high-quality print reproduction; printed on-demand anywhere in the world. This insures the ongoing accessibility of the content and helps generate sustainable revenue for the libraries and organizations that work to preserve these important materials.

The following book is in the "public domain" and represents an authentic reproduction of the text as printed by the original publisher. While we have attempted to accurately maintain the integrity of the original work, there are sometimes problems with the original work or the micro-film from which the books were digitized. This can result in minor errors in reproduction. Possible imperfections include missing and blurred pages, poor pictures, markings and other reproduction issues beyond our control. Because this work is culturally important, we have made it available as part of our commitment to protecting, preserving, and promoting the world's literature.

GUIDE TO FOLD-OUTS MAPS and OVERSIZED IMAGES

The book you are reading was digitized from microfilm captured over the past thirty to forty years. Years after the creation of the original microfilm, the book was converted to digital files and made available in an online database.

In an online database, page images do not need to conform to the size restrictions found in a printed book. When converting these images back into a printed bound book, the page sizes are standardized in ways that maintain the detail of the original. For large images, such as fold-out maps, the original page image is split into two or more pages

Guidelines used to determine how to split the page image follows:

• Some images are split vertically; large images require vertical and horizontal splits.
• For horizontal splits, the content is split left to right.
• For vertical splits, the content is split from top to bottom.
• For both vertical and horizontal splits, the image is processed from top left to bottom right.

LETTERS

WRITTEN IN

FRANCE,

IN THE SUMMER 1790,

TO A

FRIEND IN ENGLAND;

CONTAINING,

VARIOUS ANECDOTES

RELATIVE TO THE

FRENCH REVOLUTION,

AND

MEMOIRS

OF

MONS. AND MADAME DU F——

BY

HELEN MARIA WILLIAMS.

DUBLIN:

PRINTED FOR G. BURNET, P. WOGAN, P. BYRNE,
J. MOORE, J. JONES, A. GRUEBER, W. JONES,
R. WHITE, and J. RICE.

LETTERS

FROM

FRANCE.

LETTER I.

I ARRIVED at Paris, by a very rapid journey, the day before the federation; and when I am disposed to murmur at the evils of my destiny, I shall henceforth put this piece of good fortune into the opposite scale, and reflect how many disappointments it ought to counterbalance. Had the packet which conveyed me from Brighton to Dieppe sailed a few hours later; had the wind been contrary; in short, had I not reached Paris at the moment I did reach it, I should have

B   missed

miffed the moft fublime fpectacle which, perhaps, was ever reprefented on the theatre of this earth.

I fhall fend you once a week the details which I promifed when we parted, though I am well aware how very imperfectly I fhall be able to defcribe the images which prefs upon my mind. It is much eafier to feel what is fublime than to paint it; and all I fhall be able to give you will be a faint fketch, to which your own imagination muft add colouring and fpirit. The night before the federation, by way of prelude to the folemnities of that memorable day, the Te Deum was performed at the church of Notre Dame, by a greater number of muficians than have ever been affembled together, excepting at Weftminfter Abbey. The overture which preceded the Te Deum was fimple and majeftic: the mufic, highly expreffive, had the power of electrifying the hearers: and near the conclufion of the piece, the compofer, by artful difcords,

produced

produced a melancholy emotion, and then, by exciting ideas of trouble and inquietude, prepared the mind for a recitative which affected the audience in a very powerful manner, by recalling the images of that consternation and horror which prevailed in Paris on the 13th of July, 1789, the day before that on which the Baftille was taken. The words were, as well as I can recollect, what follows :—" People, your enemies advance, with hoftile fentiments, with menacing looks! They come to bathe their hands in your blood ! Already they encompafs the walls of your city ! Rife, rife from the inaction in which you are plunged, feize your arms, and fly to the combat ! God will combat with you !" Thefe words were fucceeded by a chorus of inftruments and voices, deep and folemn, which feemed to chill the foul. But what completed the effect was, when the found of a loud and heavy bell mixed itfelf with this awful concert, in imitation

of

of the alarm-bell, which, the day before
the taking of the Baftille, was rung in
every church and convent in Paris, and
which, it is faid, produced a confufion
of founds inexpreffibly horrible.   At this
moment the audience appeared to breathe
with difficulty; every heart feemed frozen
with terror ; till at lenght the bell ceafed,
the mufic changed its tone, and another
recitative announced the entire defeat of
the enemy ; and the whole terminated,
after a flourifh of drums and trumpets,
with an hymn of thankfgiving to the Supreme Being.

L E T T E R

LETTER II.

I Promifed to fend you a defcription of the federation : but it is not to be defcribed! One muft have been prefent, to form any judgment of a fcene, the fublimity of which depended much lefs on its external magnificence than on the effect it produced on the minds of the fpectators. "The people, fure, the people were the fight!" I may tell you of pavilions, of triumphal arches, of altars on which incenfe was burnt, of two hundred thoufand men walking in proceffion ; but how am I to give you an adequate idea of the behaviour of the fpectators ? How am I to paint the impetuous feelings of that immenfe, that exulting multitude ? Half a million of people affembled at a fpectacle, which furnifhed every image

B 3   that

that can elevate the mind of man; which connected the enthufiafm of moral fentiment with the folemn pomp of religious ceremonies; which addreffed itfelf at once to the imagination, the underftanding, and the heart!

The Champ de Mars was formed into an immenfe amphitheatre, round which were erected forty rows of feats, raifed one above another with earth, on which wooden forms were placed. Twenty days labour, animated by the enthufiafm of the people, accomplifhed what feemed to require the toil of years. Already in the Champ de Mars the diftinctions of rank were forgotten; and, infpired by the fame fpirit, the higheft and loweft orders of citizens gloried in taking up the fpade, and affifting the perfons employed in a work on which the common welfare of the ftate depended. Ladies took the inftruments of labour in their hands, and removed a little of the earth, that they might be able to boaft that they alfo had

affifted

affifted in the preparations at the Champ
de Mars; and a number of old foldiers
were feen voluntarily beftowing on their
country the laft remains of their ftrength.
A young Abbé of my acquaintance told
me, that the people beat a drum at the
door of the convent where he lived, and
obliged the Superior to let all the Monks
come out and work in the Champ de
Mars. The Superior with great reluctance acquiefced, " Quant à moi," faid
the young Abbé, " je ne demandois pas
mieux*."

At the upper end of the amphitheatre
a pavilion was built for the reception of
the King, the Queen, their attendants,
and the National Affembly, covered with
ftriped tent-cloth of the national colours,
and decorated with ftreamers of the fame
beloved tints, and fleurs. de lys. The
white flag was difplayed above the fpot
where the King was feated. In the middle of the Champ de Mars L'Autel de la

* As for me, I defired nothing better.

Patrie

Patrie was placed, on which incenfe was burnt by priefts dreffed in long white robes, with fafhes of national ribbon. Several infcriptions were written on the altar, but the words vifible at the greateft diftance were, La Nation, la Loi, et le Roi*.

At the lower end of the amphitheatre, oppofite to the pavilion, three triumphal arches were erected, adorned with emblems and allegorical figures.

The proceffion marched to the Champ de Mars, through the central ftreets of Paris. At La Place de Louis Quinze, the efcorts, who carried the colours, received under their banners, ranged in two lines, the National Affembly, who came from the Tuilleries. When the proceffion paffed the ftreet where Henry the Fourth was affaffinated, every man paufed as if by general confent: the cries of joy were fufpended, and fucceeded by a folemn filence. This tribute of regret,

* The Nation, the Law, and the King

paid

paid from the fudden impulfe of feeling at fuch a moment, was perhaps the moft honourable teftimony to the virtues of that amiable Prince which his memory has yet received.

In the ftreets, at the windows, and on the roofs of the houfes, the people, tranf-ported with joy, fhouted and wept as the proceffion paffed. Old men were feen kneeling in the ftreets, bleffing God that they had lived to witnefs that happy moment. The people ran to the doors of their houfes loaded with refrefhments, which they offered to the troops; and crouds of women furrounded the foldiers, and holding up their infants in their arms, and melting into tears, promifed to make their children imbibe, from their earlieft age, an inviolable attachment to the prin-ciples of the new conftitution.

The proceffion entered the Champ de Mars by a long road, which thoufands of people had affifted in forming, by filling up deep hollows, levelling the rifing grounds,

grounds, and erecting a temporary bridge
acrofs the Seine, oppofite to the triumphal arches.   The order of the proceffion
was as follows:

A troop of horfe, with trumpets.

A great band of mufic.

A detachment of grenadiers.

The electors chofen at Paris in 1789.

A band of volunteers.

The affembly of the reprefentatives of
   the people.

The military committee.

Company of chaffeurs.

A band of drums.

The Prefidents of fixty diftricts.

The Deputies of the people fent to the
   Federation.

The Adminiftrators of the municipa-
   lity.

Bands of mufic and drums.

Battalion of children, carrying a ftand-
   ard, on which was written, L'Efpe-
   rance de la Patrie *.

* The Hope of the Country.

Detachment

Detachment with the colours of the
national guard of Paris.

Battalion of veterans.

Deputies from forty-two departments,
arranged alphabetically.

The Oriflamme, or grand ſtandard of
the Kings of France.

Deputies from the regular troops.

Deputies from the navy.

Deputies from forty-one departments,
arranged alſo alphabetically.

Band of volunteer chaſſeurs.

Troop of horſe, with trumpets.

The proceſſion, which was formed with
eight perſons abreaſt, entered the Champ
de Mars beneath the triumphal arches,
with a diſcharge of cannon. The deputies placed themſelves round the inſide
of the amphitheatre. Between them and
the ſeats of the ſpectators, the national
guard of Paris were ranged; and the
ſeats round the amphitheatre were filled
with four hundred thouſand people. The
middle of the amphitheatre was crouded
with

with an immense multitude of foldiers.
The National Affembly walked towards
the pavilion, where they placed themfelves
with the King, the Queen, the royal family, and their attendants; and oppofite
this group, rofe in perfpective the hills
of Paffy and Chaillot, covered with people. The ftandards, of which one was
prefented to each department of the kingdom, as a mark of brotherhood, by the
citizens of Paris, were carried to the
altar to be confecrated by the bifhop.
High mafs was performed, after which
Monfieur de la Fayette, who had been
appointed by the King Major General of
the Federation, afcended the altar, gave
the fignal, and himfelf took the national
oath. In an inftant every fword was
drawn, and every arm lifted up. The
King pronounced the oath, which the
Prefident of the National Affembly repeated, and the folemn words were re-
echoed by fix hundred thoufand voices;
while the Queen raifed th e Dauphin in her

arms

arms, fhewing him to the people and the army. At the moment the confecrated banners were difplayed, the fun, which had been obfcured by frequent fhowers in the courfe of the morning; burft forth, while the people lifted their eyes to heaven, and called upon the Deity to look down and witnefs the facred engagement into which they entered. A refpectful filence was fucceeded by the cries, the fhouts, the acclamations of the multitude: they wept, they embraced each other, and then difperfed.

You will not fufpect that I was an indifferent witnefs of fuch a fcene. Oh no! this was not a time in which the diftinctions of country were remembered. It was the triumph of human kind; it was man afferting the nobleft privileges of his nature; and it required but the common feelings of humanity to become in that moment a citizen of the world. For myfelf, I acknowledge that my heart caught with enthufiafm the general fympathy;

my

my eyes were filled with tears; and I shall never forget the fenfations of that day, " while memory holds her feat in my " bofom."

The weather proved very unfavourable during the morning of the federation; but the minds of people were too much elevated by ideas of moral good, to attend to the phyfical evils of the day. Several heavy fhowers were far from interrupting the general gaiety. The people, when drenched by the rain, called out with exultation, rather than regret, * " Nous fommes mouillez a la nation." Some exclaimed, †" La revolution Françoife eft cimentée avec de l'eau, au lieu de fang." The national guard, during the hours which preceded the arrival of the proceffion, amufed the fpectators ‡ d'une dance ronde, and with a thoufand

* We are wet for the nation.

† The French revolution is cemented with water, inftead of blood.

‡ With dancing in a circle.

whimfical

whimfical and playful evolutions, highly
expreffive of that gaiety which diftin-
guifhes the French character. I believe
none but Frenchmen would have diverted
themfelves, and half a million of people,
who were waiting in expectation of a fcene
the moft folemn upon record, by circles
of ten thoufand men galloping * en dance
ronde. But if you are difpofed to think
of this gaiety with the contempt of fuperior gravity, for I will not call it wifdom,
recollect that thefe dancers were the very
men whofe bravery formed the great epocha of French liberty; the heroes who
demolifhed the towers of the Baftille, and
whofe fame will defcend to the lateft pofterity.

Such was the admirable order with
which this auguft fpectacle was conducted, that no accident interrupted the univerfal feftivity. All carriages were forbidden during that day; and the entrances
to the Champ de Mars were fo nume-

* In the round dance.

rous,

rous, that half a milion of people were collected together without a croud.

The people had only one subject of regret: they murmured that the king had taken the national oath in the pavilion, inftead of performing that ceremony at the foot of the altar; and fome of them crouding round Monf. de la Fayette, conjured him to perfuade the king to go to the altar, and take the oath a fecond time. * " Mes enfans," faid Monf. de la Fayette, " le ferment n'eft pas une ariette, on ne peut pas le jouer deux fois."

Monf. de la Fayette, after the Federation, went to the Chateau de la Muette, where a public dinner was prepared for the national guard. An immenfe croud gathered round him when he alighted from his horfe, at a little diftance from the chateau, and fome Ariftocrates, mixing themfelves with the true worfhippers of

* My friends, the oath is not an air which can be played twice over.

him

him who is so justly the idol of the French nation, attempted to stifle him with their embraces. He called out " † *Mais, mes amis, vous m'etouffez!*" and one of his *aide de camps*, who perceived the danger of his general, threw himself from his horse, which he intreated Monf. de la Fayette to mount. He did so, and hastened to the chateau.

This incident reminds me of a line in Racine's fine tragedy of Britannicus, where Nero says,

† " J'embrasse mon rival, mais c'est pour l'etouffer."

Adieu.

---

* But, my friends, you stifle me.
† I embrace my rival, but it is to destroy him.

LETTER

LETTER III.

THE rejoicings at Paris did not terminate with the ceremony of the Federation. A fucceffion of entertainments, which lafted feveral days, were prepared for the deputies from the provinces, who were all quartered in the houfes of the bourgeois, where they were received with the moft cordial hofpitality.

The night of the 14th of July the whole city of Paris was illuminated, and the next day le ci-devant Duc, now Monf. d'Orleans, gave a public dinner to the national guard in the hall of the Palais Royal. We walked in the evening round the gallery, from which we faw part of the croud below amufing themfelves by dancing, while others were finging in chorus the favourite national fongs.

On

On the following Sunday the national guards were reviewed by Monf. de la Fayette in the Champ de Mars, which was again filled with fpectators, and the people appeared more enthufiaftic than ever in their applaufes of their general. The Champ de Mars refounded with re-peated cries of * " Vive Monf. de la Fay-ette." On this day carriages were again forbidden, and the evening difplayed a fcene of general rejoicing. The whole city was illuminated, and crouds of com-pany filled the gardens of the Tuilleries, from which we faw the beautiful façade of the Louvre lighted in the moft fplen-did manner. In the Champs Elyfées, where a fête was given to the Deputies, innumerable lamps were hung from one row of trees to another, and fhed the moft agreeable brilliance on thofe enchanting walks; where the exhilarated croud danced and fung, and filled the air with the found of rejoicing. Several parties of the na-

* Long live Monf. de la Fayette.

tional

tional guard came from the Champ Elyfées, dancing along the walks of the Tuilleries with a woman between every two
men; and all the priests, whom they met
in their way, they obliged to join in the
dance, treating them as women, by placing them between two foldiers, and fometimes fportively drefling them in grenadiers caps. Fire-works of great variety
and beauty were exhibited on the Pont
Neuf, and the ftatue of Henry the Fourth
was decorated with the ornament of all
others the moft dear in the eyes of the
people, a fcarf of national ribbon. Trans-
parencies of Monf. de la Fayette and
Monf. Bailly were placed, as the higheft
mark of public favour, on each fide of
this revered ftatue.

But the fpectacle of all others the moft
interefting to my feelings, was the rejoicings at the Baftille. The ruins of that
execrable fortrefs were fuddenly tranf-
formed, as if with the wand of necro-
mancy, into a fcene of beauty and of pleafure.

fure. The ground was covered with freſh
clods of graſs, upon which young trees
were placed in rows, and illuminated with
a blaze of light. Here the minds of the
people took a higher tone of exultation
than in the other ſcenes of feſtivity. Their
mutual congratulations, their reflections
on the horror of the paſt, their ſenſe of
preſent felicity, their cries of * " Vive la
Nation," ſtill ring in my ear! I too, though
but a ſojourner in their land, rejoiced in
their happineſs, joined the univerſal voice,
and repeated with all my heart and ſoul,
" Vive la nation!"

* Long live the Nation.

LETTER

LETTER IV.

BEFORE I suffered my friends at Paris to conduct me through the usual routine of convents, churches, and palaces, I requested to visit the Bastille; feeling a much stronger desire to contemplate the ruins of that building than the most perfect edifices of Paris. When we got into the carriage, our French servant called to the coachman with an air of triumph, * "A la Bastille mais nous n'y resterons pas." We drove under that porch which so many wretches have entered never to repass, and alighting from the carriage descended with difficulty into the dungeons, which were too low to admit of our standing upright, and so dark that we were obliged at noon-day to visit them

* To the Bastile,—but we shall not remain there.

with

with the light of a candle. We saw the
hooks of those chains by which the prisoners were fastened round the neck, to
the walls of their cells; many of which
being below the level of the water, are in
a constant state of humidity; and a nox-
ious vapour issued from them, which
more than once extinguished the candle,
and was so insufferable that it required a
strong spirit of curiosity to tempt one to
enter. Good God!—and to these regions
of horror were human creatures dragged
at the caprice of despotic power. What
a melancholy consideration, that

> ———— " Man! proud man,
> Drest in a little brief authority,
> Plays such fantastic tricks before high heaven;
> As make the angels weep "————

There appears to be a greater number
of these dungeons than one could have
imagined the hard heart of tyranny itself
would contrive; for, since the destruction
of the building, many subterraneous cells
have been discovered underneath a piece

of

of ground which was inclofed within the walls of the Baftille, but which feemed a bank of folid earth before the horrid fe- crets of this prifon-houfe were difclofed. Some fkeletons were found in thefe re- ceffes, with irons ftill faftened on their decaying bones.

After having vifited the Baftille, we may indeed be furprized, that a nation fo enlightened as the French, fubmitted fo long to the oppreffions of their govern- ment ; but we muft ceafe to wonder that their indignant fpirits at length fhook off the galling yoke.

Thofe who have contemplated the dun- geons of the Baftille, without rejoicing in the French revolution, may, for ought I know, be very refpectable perfons, and very agreeable companions in the hours of profperity ; but, if my heart were fink- ing with anguifh, I fhould not fly to thofe perfons for confolation. Sterne fays, that a man is incapable of loving one woman

as he ought, who has not a fort of an affection for the whole fex; and as little
fhould I look for particular fympathy
from thofe who have no feelings of general philanthropy. If the fplendour of a
defpotic throne can only fhine like the ra-
diance of lightning, while all around is involved in gloom and horror, in the name
of heaven let its baleful luftre be extinguifhed for ever. May no fuch ftrong
contraft of light and fhade again exift in
the political fyftem of France! but may
the beams of liberty, like the beams of
day, fhed their benign influence on the
cottage of the peafant, as well as on the
palace of the monarch! May liberty,
which for fo many ages paft has taken
pleafure in foftening the evils of the bleak
and rugged climates of the north, in fer-
tilizing a barren foil, in clearing the
fwamp, in lifting mounds againft the inun-
dations of the tempeft, diffufe her bleffings alfo on the genial land of France,

C   and

and bid the hufbandman rejoice under the fhade of the olive and the vine!

The Baftille, which Henry the Fourth and his veteran troops affailed in vain, the citizens of Paris had the glory of taking in a few hours The avarice of Monf. de Launay had tempted him to guard this fortrefs with only half the complement of men ordered by government; and a letter which he received the morning of the 14th of July, commanding him to fuftain the fiege till the evening, when fuccour would arrive, joined to his own treachery towards the affailants, coft him his life

The courage of the befiegers was inflamed by the horrors of famine, there being at this time only twenty-four hours provifion of bread in Paris. For fome days the people had affembled in crouds round the fhops of the bakers, who were obliged to have a guard of foldiers to protect them from the famifhed multitude; while the women, rendered furious

by

by want, cried, in the resolute tone of despair, * "Il nous faut du pain pour nos enfans." Such was the scarcity of bread, that a French gentleman told me, that, the day preceding the taking of the Bastille, he was invited to dine with a Negotiant, and, when he went, was informed that a servant had been out five hours in search of bread, and had at last been able to purchase only one loaf.

It was at this crisis, it was to save themselves the shocking spectacle of their wives and infants perishing before their eyes, that the citizens of Paris flew to arms, and, impelled by such causes, fought with the daring intrepidity of men who had all that renders life of any value at stake, and who determined to die or conquer. The women too, far from indulging the fears incident to our feeble sex, in defiance of the cannon of the Bastille, ventured to bring victuals to their sons and

* We must have bread for our children.

husbands;

hufbands; and, with a fpirit worthy of Roman matrons, encouraged them to go on. Women mounted guard in the ftreets, and when any perfon paffed, called out boldly, * " Qui va la?

A gentleman, who had the command of fifty men in this enterprize, told me, that one of his foldiers being killed by a cannon-ball, the people, with great marks of indignation, removed the corpfe, and then, fnatching up the dead man's hat, begged money of the byftanders for his interment, in a manner characteriftic enough of that gaiety, which never for-fakes the French, even on fuch occafions as would make any other people on earth ferious. † " Madame, pour ce pauvre diable qui fe fait tué pour la Nation! —Monf. pour ce pauvre chien qui fe fait tué pour la nation!" This mode of

* Who goes there?

† Madam, for this poor devil, who has been kill_d for the nation!—Sir, for this unfortunate dog, who has been killed for the Nation!

fupplication,

fupplication, though not very pathetic, obtained the end defired; no perfon being fufficiently obdurate to refift the powerful plea, * " qu'il fe fait tué pour la Nation."

When the Baftille was taken, and the old man, of whom you have no doubt heard, and who had been confined in a dungeon thirty-five years, was brought into day light, which had not for fo long a fpace of time vifited his eyes, he ftaggered fhook his white beard, and cried faintly, † " Meffieurs, vous m'avez rendu un grand fervice, rendez m'en un autre, tuez moi! je ne fais pas où aller."—" Allons, allons," the croud anfwered with one voice, " la Nation te nourrira."

As the heroes of the Baftille paffed along the ftreets after its furrender, the

* Had been killed for the Nation.

† Gentlemen, you have rendered me one great fervice; render me another, kill me! for I know not where to go.—Come along, come along, the Nation will provide for you.

C 3　　　　citizens

citizens ſtood at the doors of their houſes loaded with wine, brandy, and other re-freſhments, which they offered to theſe deliverers of their country. But they unanimouſly refuſed to taſte any ſtrong liquors, conſidering the great work they had undertaken as not yet accompliſhed, and being determined to watch the whole night, in caſe of any ſurprize.

All thoſe who had aſſiſted in taking the Baſtille, were preſented by the municipa-lity of Paris with a ribbon of the national colours, on which is ſtamped, incloſed in a circle of braſs, an impreſſion of the Baſtille, and which is worn as a military order.

The municipality of Paris alſo pro-poſed a ſolemn funeral proceſſion in me-mory of thoſe who loſt their lives in this enterprize; but, on making application to the National Aſſembly for a deputation of its members to aſſiſt at this ſolemnity, the Aſſembly were of opinion that theſe funeral honours ſhould be poſtponed till a

more

more favourable moment, as they might at prefent have a tendency to inflame the minds of the people.

I have heard feveral perfons mention a young man, of a little infignificant figure, who, the day before the Baftille was taken, got up on a chair in the Palais Royal, and harangued the multitude, conjuring them to make a ftruggle for their liberty, and afferting, that now the moment was arrived. They liftened to his eloquence with the moft eager attention; and, when he had inftructed as many as could hear him at one time, he requefted them to depart, and repeated his harangue to a new fet of auditors.

Among the dungeons of the Baftille are placed, upon a heap of ftones, the figures of the two men who contrived the plan of this fortrefs, where they were afterwards confined for life. Thefe men are reprefented chained to the wall, and are beheld without any emotion of fympathy.

The

The perſon employed to remove the ruins of the Baſtille, has framed of the ſtones eighty-three complete models of this building, which, with a true patri- otic ſpirit, he has preſented to the eighty- three departments of the kingdom, by way of hint to his countrymen to take care of their liberties in future.

LETTER

LETTER V.

I Am juſt returned from a viſit to Madame *Sillery*, whoſe works on education are ſo well known and ſo juſtly eſteemed in England, and who received me with the moſt engaging politeneſs. Surely the French are unrivalled in the arts of pleaſing; in the power of uniting with the moſt poliſhed elegance of manners, that attentive kindneſs which ſeems to flow warm from the heart, and which, while it ſooths our vanity, ſecures our affections. Madame Sillery and her pupils are at preſent at St. Leu, a beautiful ſpot in the rich valley of Montmorenci. Monſ. d' Orleans has certainly conferred a moſt eſſential obligation upon his children, by placing them under the care of this lady. I never met with young people

ple

ple more amiable in their difpofitions, or
more charming in their manners, which
are equally remote from arrogance, and
from thofe efforts of condefcenfion which
I have feen fome great people make,
with much difficulty to themfelves, and
much offence to others. The Princefs,
who is thirteen years of age, has a countenance of the fweeteft expreffion, and
appears to me to be Adelaide the heroine
of Madame Sillery's Letters on education,
perfonified. The three princes, though
under Madame Sillery's fuperintendence,
have alfo preceptors who live in the
houfe, and affift in their education. The
eldeft prince, Monf. de Chartres, is
nearly eighteen years of age, and his
attentive politenefs formed a ftriking
contraft in my mind, to the manners of
thofe fafhionable gentlemen in a certain
great metropolis, who confider apathy
and negligence as the teft of good breed-
ing. But if I was pleafed with the manners of this young Prince, I was ftill more
delighted

delighted to find him a confirmed friend
to the new constitution of France, and
willing, with the enthusiasm of a young
and ardent mind, to renounce the splendour of his titles for the general good.
When he heard that the sacrifice of
fortune also was required, and that the
immense property, which he had been
taught to consider as his inheritance, was
to be divided with his brothers, he embraced them with the utmost affection,
declaring that he should rejoice in such a
division. To find a democratic Prince,
was somewhat singular : I was much less
surprized that Madame Sillery had adopted sentiments which are so congenial to
an enlarged and comprehensive mind.
This lady I have called Sillery, because it
is the name by which she is known in
England ; but, since the decree of the National Assembly, abolishing the nobility,
she has renounced with her title the name
of Sillery, and has taken that of Brulart.

She

She talked to me of the diftinctions of rank, in the fpirit of philofophy, and ridiculed the abfurdity of converting the rewards of perfonal merit into the inheritance of thofe who had perhaps fo little claim to honours, that they were a fort of oblique reproach on their character and conduct. There may be arguments againft hereditary rank fufficiently convincing to fuch an underftanding as Madame Brulart's: but I know fome French ladies who entertain very different notions on this fubject; who fee no impropriety in the eftablifhments of nobility; and who have carried their love of ariftocratical rights fo far as to keep their beds, in a fit of defpondency, upon being obliged to relinquifh the agreeable epithets of Comteffe or Marquife, to which their ears had been fo long accuftomed.

But let me do juftice to the ladies of France. The number of thofe who have murmured at the lofs of rank, bears a very

fmall

fmall proportion to thofe who have acted
with a fpirit of diftinguifhed patriotifm;
who, with thofe generous affections which
belong to the female heart, have gloriedin
facrificing titles, fortune, and even the perfonal ornaments, fo dear to female vanity,
for the common caufe. It was the ladies
who gave the example of le don patriotique*, by offering their jewels at the
fhrine of liberty; and, if the women of
ancient Rome have gained the applaufe of
diftant ages for fuch actions, the women
of France will alfo claim the admiration
of pofterity.

The women have certainly had a confiderable fhare in the French revolution:
for, whatever the imperious lords of the
creation may fancy, the moft important
events which take place in this world de-
pend a little on our influence; and we
often act in human affairs like thofe fecret

* The patriotic donation.

fprings

springs in mechanism, by which, though invisible, great movements are regulated.

But let us return to Madame Brulart, who wears at her breast a medallion made of a stone of the Bastille polished. In the middle of the medallion, *Liberté* was written in diamonds; above was marked in diamonds, the planet that shone on the 14th of July; and below was seen the moon, of the size she appeared that memorable night. The medallion was set in a branch of laurel, composed of emeralds, and tied at the top with the national cockade, formed of brilliant stones of the three national colours.

Our conversation on the subject of the Bastille, led Madame Brulart to relate an action of Monf. de Chartres, which reflects the highest honour on his humanity. Being in Normandy, he visited Mont St. Michel, a fortress built on a rock which stands a league and a half from the coast of Normandy. The tide covers this space

twice

twice every twenty-four hours but when
it is low-water, a perſon can paſs over on
foot. Mont St. Michel was originally a
church, founded by a good biſhop in the
ſeventh century, in honour of St. Michel,
who, it ſeems, appeared to him in a viſion
on this ſpot. Richard, the firſt Duke of
Normandy of that name, afterwards converted the church into an abbey, and this
abbey gave riſe to the military order des
Chevaliers de St. Michel, inſtituted by
Louis the Eleventh. After having ſeen the
precious relics of the abbey, the ſquare
buckler, and the ſhort ſword found in
Ireland near the body of the well-known
dragon, whoſe deſtruction is attributed to
the prowefs of St. Michel, Monſ. de Chartres was conducted, through many laby-
rinths, to the ſubterraneous parts of the
edifice; where he was ſhewn a wooden
cage, which was made by order of Louis
the Fourteenth, for the puniſhment of an
unfortunate wit, who had dared to ridi-
cule

cule his conquefts in Holland, no fooner
gained than loft. Monf. de Chartres,
beheld with horror this ~inftrument of
tyranny, in which prifoners were ftill
frequently confined; and, expreffing in
very ftrong terms his indignation. he was
told, that, as a prince of the blood, he
had a right, if he thought proper, to
order the cage to be deftroyed. Scarcely
were the words pronounced, when the
young Prince feized a hatchet, gave the
firft ftroke himfelf to this execrable machine, waited to fee it levelled with the
ground, and thus may claim the glory of
having, even before the demolition of the
Baftille, begun the French revolution.

We found at St. Leu a young Englifh
lady, who is the companion of the Princefs, and whofe appearance is calculated
to give the moft favourable idea of Englifh beauty. I never faw more regular
features, or an expreffion of countenance
more lovely: and Madame Brulart, by
whom fhe has been educated, affured me

that

that " the mind keeps the promiſe we had from the face." This young lady talked of her own country with a glow of ſatisfaction very grateful to my feelings. She ſeems to,

" Caſt a look where England's glories ſhine,
" And bids her boſom ſympathiſe with mine."

LETTER

LETTER VI.

I Have been at the National Affembly,
where, at a time when the deputies from
the provinces engroffed every ticket of
admiffion, my fifter and I were admited
without tickets, by the gentleman who
had the command of the guard, and placed
in the beft feats, before he fuffered the
doors to be opened to other people. We
had no perfonal acquaintance with this
gentleman, or any claim to his politenefs,
except that of being foreigners and women; but thefe are, of all claims, the
moft powerful to the urbanity of French
manners

My fifter obferved to me, that our feats,
which were immediately oppofite the tribune from which the members fpeak, re-
minded her of our ftruggles to attain the
                                        fame

fame fituation in Weftminfter Hall. But
you muft recollect, I anfwered, that we
have attained this fituation without any
ftruggle. I believe, however, that if the
fame of Mr. Fox's eloquence fhould lead
a French woman to prefent herfelf at the
door of Weftminfter Hall without a ticket, fhe might ftand there as long as Mr.
Haftings's trial has lafted, without being
permitted to pafs the barrier.

The hall of the National Affembly is
long and narrow; at each end there is a
gallery, where the common people are
admitted by applying very early in the
morning for numbers, which are diftri-
buted at the door; and the perfons
who firft apply fecure the firft numbers.
The feats being alfo numbered, all confufion and diforder are prevented The
galleries at the fide of the hall are divided into boxes, which are called tri-
bunes. They belong to the principal
members of the National Affembly, and
to

to thefe places company are admitted
with tickets. Rows of feats are placed
round the hall, raifed one above another,
where the members of the Affembly are
feated; and immediately oppofite the chair
of the prefident, in the narrow part of
the hall, is the tribune which the members afcend when they are going to fpeak.
One capital fubject of debate in this Affembly is, who fhall fpeak firft; for all
feem more inclined to talk than to liften;
and fometimes the prefident in vain rings
a bell, or with the vehemence of French
action ftretches out his arms, and endeavours to impofe filence; while the fix
Huiffers, perfons who are appointed to
keep order, make the attempt with as
little fuccefs as the prefident himfelf. But
one ceafes to wonder that the meetings of
the National Affembly are tumultuous,
on reflecting how important are the objects of its deliberations. Not only the
lives and fortunes of individuals, but the
exiftence

existence of the country is at stake: and of how little consequence is this impetuosity in debate, if the decrees which are passed are wise and beneficial, and the new constitution arises, like the beauty and order of nature, from the confusion of mingled elements! I heard several of the members speak; but I am so little qualified to judge of oratory, that, without presuming to determine whether I had reason to be entertained or not, I shall only tell you that I was so.

And this, repeated I with exultation to myself, this is the National Assembly of France! Those men now before my eyes are the men who engross the attention, the astonishment of Europe; for the issue of whose decrees surrounding nations wait in suspence, and whose fame has already extended through every civilized region of the globe: the men whose magnanimity invested them with power to destroy the old constitution, and whose wisdom is

erecting

erecting the new, on a principle of perfection which has hitherto been thought chimerical, and has only ferved to adorn the page of the philofopher; but which they believe may be reduced to practice, and have therefore the courage to attempt. My mind, with a fenfation of elevated pleafure, paffing through the interval of ages, anticipated the increafing renown of thefe legiflators, and the period when, all the nations of Europe following the liberal fyftem which France has adopted, the little crooked policy of the prefent times fhall give place to the reign of reafon, virtue, and fcience.

The moft celebrated characters in the National Affembly were pointed out to us. Monfieur Barnave de Dauphiné, who is only fix and twenty years of age, and the youngeft member of the Affembly, is efteemed its firft orator, and is the leader of the democratic party. I believe Monf. Barnave does not owe all his reputation

putation to his talents, however diftinguifhed: his virtues alfo claim a confiderable fhare of that applaufe which he re-
ceives from his country. He has fhewn
himfelf as ftedfaft in principle, as he is
eloquent in debate. With firm undevi-
ating integrity he has defended the caufe
of the people. Every motion he has
made in the Affembly has paffed into a
law, becaufe its beneficial tendency has
been always evident; and it was he who
effected that memorable decree which
deprived the King of the power of making war, without the confent of the nation. Monf. Bārnave is adored by the
people; who have two or three times taken the horfes from his carriage, and
drawn him in triumph along the ftreets
of Paris.

We alfo faw Monf Mirabeau l'ainé,
whofe genius is of the firft clafs, but who
poffefles a very fmall fhare of popularity.
I am, however, one of his partizans,
though

though not merely from that enthusiasm
which always comes across my heart in
favour of great intellectual abilities Monf.
Mirabeau has another very powerful claim
on my partiality: he is the professed friend
(and I must and will love him for being
so) of the African race.   He has pro-
posed the abolition of the slave trade to
the National Assembly, and, though the
Assembly have delayed the consideration
of this subject, on account of those deliberations which immediately affect the
country, yet, perhaps, if our senators continue to doze over this affair as they have
hitherto done, the French will have the
glory of setting us an example, which it
will then be our humble employment to
follow.   But I trust the period will never
come, when England will submit to be
taught by another nation the lesson of humanity.   I trust an English House of
Commons will never persist in thinking,
that what is morally wrong, can be poli-
tically

tically right; that the virtue and the prosperity of a people are things at variance with each other; and that a country which abounds with so many sources of wealth, cannot afford to close one polluted channel, which is stained with the blood of our fellow-creatures.

But it is a sort of treason to the honour, the spirit, the generosity of Englishmen, to suppose they will persevere in such conduct. Admitting, however, a supposition which it is painful to make; admitting that they should abide by this system of inhumanity, they will only retard, but will not finally prevent the abolition of slavery. The Africans have not long to suffer, nor their oppressors to triumph. Europe is hastening towards a period too enlightened for the perpetuation of such monstrous abuses. The mists of ignorance and error are rolling fast away, and the benign beams of philosophy are spreading their lustre over the nations.—But

D whither

whither have thefe children of captivity led me? I perceive I have wandered a great way from the National Affembly, where I was fo happily feated, and of which I will tell you more in my next letter

LETTER

LETTER. VII.

THE Abbé Maury is one of the most distinguished members of the National Assembly. He possesses astonishing powers of eloquence; but he has done his talents the injustice to make them subservient to the narrow considerations of self-interest. Had he displayed that ability in defence of civil and religious liberty, which he has employed in the service of the exorbitant pretentions of the church, he would have deserved the highest applause of his country; instead of which, he has called to the aid of his genius an auxiliary it ought to have scorned; that subtlety which tries " to make the worse appear the better reason;" and he is still more detested than admired. I am not surprized that a little mind is sometimes tempted by interest to tread in t

D 2 mean

mean and fordid path; but I own it does aftonifh me that genius can be feduced from the fair field of honourable fame into thofe ferpentine ways where it can meet with no object worthy of its ambi-tion. " Something too much of this." You fhall hear a repartee of the Abbé Maury, who, after having made a very unpopular motion in the Affembly, was infulted as he was going out; the people crying, as they are too apt to do, * " A la lanterne." The Abbé, turning to the croud, anfwered, with equal indignation and fpirit, † " Eh! Meffieurs, fi j'etois à la lanterne, feriez vous plus eclairés?" The Abbé Maury, before the revolution, was in poffeffion of eight hundred farms, and has loft fixty thoufand livres a year in confequence of that event. But enough

* To the lantern.

† If I were at the lantern, would you be more enlightened?

of

of Monf. l'Abbé, whofe picture I have juft purchafed in a fnuff-box. You touch a fpring, open the lid of the. fnuff box, and the Abbé jumps up, and occafions much furprize and merriment. The joke, however, is grown a little ftale in France: but I fhall bring the Abbé with me to England, where l flatter myfelf his fudden appearance will afford fome diverfion.

A fingular but very refpectable figure in the National Affembly is a Deputy from Britanny, called Le Pere Gerard. This venerable old man is a peafant, and his appearance reminds one of thofe times when Generals were called from the plough to take the command of armies. The drefs of Le Pere Gerard is made of a coarfe wollen cloth, which is worn by the peafants of Britanny, and is of fuch ftrong texture that a coat often defcends from one generation to another. This cloth is called Pinchina; and the King, to whom the old Breton has prefented feveral

D 3 addreffes

addreffes from the Affembly, calls him, * en badinage, Le Pere Pinchina. When I faw him, he had on this everlafting coat, and wore worfted ftockings gartered above the knees. But, what pleafed me moft in his appearance, were the long white hairs which hung down his fhoulders; an ornament for which you know I have a particular predilection.

The refpectable Pere Gerard boafts that he is defcended from a race of deputies, his great grandfather having been chofen as a deputy to Les Etats Generaux in 1614, the laft time the States were held, before that memorable period when they effected the revolution.

At the time when the ladies fet the example of † Le don patrioque, by offering their jewels, and the members of the National Affembly, in a moment of enthu-

* In pleafantry, Father Pinchina.

† The patriotic donation.

fiafm

fiafm, took the filver buckles out of their
fhoes, and laid them on the Prefident's
table, the Pere Gerard arofe, and faid, that
he had no fuch offering to give, his buckles
being made of brafs, but that his don patriotique fhould be that of rendering his
fervices to his country unpaid. The old
man was heard by the Affembly with the
applaufe he merited; and the people, on
the day of the Federation, carried him
from the Champ de Mars to his own
houfe in triumph on their fhoulders.

Meffieurs Charles and Alexander La-
meth, two brothers, and Monf. Rabeau
de St. Eftienne, are among the firft pa-
triots of the National Affembly, and have
a very high reputation for talents. The
French, who love what they call an
* equivoque, tell you, que Monf. Rabeau
vaut deux d'Mirabeau.

The meetings of the Affembly, though
ftill tumultuous, are much lefs fo than

* A play upon words.

they

they were at their firſt commencement.
A gentleman, who was preſent when the
motion was made for aboliſhing monaſte-
ries, told me, that the minds of the members were, on that occaſion, inflamed to
ſuch a height, that it appeared to him
very probable, that the debate would end
in a maſſacre. He mentioned a circum-
ſtance very characteriſtic of French vivacity. One of the members was expreſſing
himſelf in theſe words, " What is a Monk?
A man who has renounced his father, his
mother, every tie, every affection that is
dear in nature! and for whom?"—before
the ſpeaker could finiſh his ſentence, a
member from the other end of the hall
ſeized the moment while the orator was
drawing his breath, and called out * " Pour
une puiſſance etrangere," to the great
horror of la coté noir, for ſo the clergy
are called.

* For a foreign power.

The

The Democrates place themſelves on one ſide of the hall, and the Ariſtocrates on the other. The ſpectators in the galleries take ſuch a part in the debate, as frequently to expreſs their applauſe by clapping their hands with great violence. An old Marechal of France roſe, the day I was at the Aſſembly, when they were debating on the military penſions, and declared, that in recompence for the ſervices which he had rendered his country, he deſired honours and not pay. The Aſſembly clapped him, and the galleries joined in this mark of approbation. A young Frenchman, who ſat next me, whiſpered to me, *" Monſ. trouve apparament que l'argent l'incommode."

The members of the National Aſſembly are paid three crowns a day for their attendance; while in England a candidate for a ſeat in parliament often ſpends

* I ſuppoſe that gentleman finds money troubleſome.

many

many thoufand pounds, and, with magnificent generofity, makes a whole coun-
ty drunk for a week, merely to enjoy the
privilege of ferving his country without
pay.

The qualification requifite for a member of the National Affembly, is that of
poffeffing fufficient property in land or
houfes to pay taxes to the amount of a
marc d'argent, which is the value of four
louis. Every hundred of the citizens, who
pay taxes to government of three days
labour, or three livres, have a right to
vote for an electer, whofe qualification is
that of paying taxes to the amount of ten
livres, or ten days labour. The electors
of one department meet together in one
affembly, and chufe from among their
own body the perfons who are to direct
the adminiftration of that department.
Thofe electors will alfo chufe in the fame
manner the deputies fent by that department to the National Affembly. There
will therefore be only one intermediate
degree

degree between the lowest order of active citizens, and the members of the National Assembly.

I was interrupted by a visitor, who related a little incident, which has interested me so much, that I can write of nothing else at present, and you shall therefore have it warm from my heart. While the National Assembly were deliberating upon the division of property among brothers, a young man of high birth and fortune, who is a member of the Assembly, entered with precipitation, and, mounting the tribune, with great emotion informed the Assembly, that he had just received account that his father was dying; that he himself was his eldest son, and had come to conjure the Assembly to pass, without delay, that equitable decree, giving the younger sons an equal share of fortune with the eldest, in order, he said, that his father might have the satisfaction, before he breathed his last, of knowing that all his children were secure of a provision.

If

If you are not affected by this circum-
stance, you have read it with very different feelings from those with which I have
written it: but if, on the contrary, you
have fallen in love with this young Frenchman, do not imagine your passion is singular, for I am violently in love with him
myself.

LETTER

LETTER VIII.

YOU have not heard, perhaps. that on the day of the Federation at Paris, the national oath was taken throughout the whole kingdom. at the hour of twelve.

A great number of farmers and peasants walked in the proceſſion at Rouen, bearing in their hands the inſtruments of their huſbandry, decorated with national ribbons. The national guard cut down branches from the trees, and ſtuck them in their hats; and a French gentleman of my acquaintance, who underſtands Engliſh, and reads Shakeſpeare, told me that it ſeemed like Birnham Wood coming to Dunſinane.

The leaders of the French revolution, are men well acquainted with the human heart. They have not truſted merely to the

the force of reason, but have studied to
interest in their cause the most powerful
passions of human nature, by the appointment of solemnities perfectly calculated to awaken that general sympathy
which is caught from heart to heart with
irresistible energy, fills every eye with
tears, and dissolves every bosom

I have heard of a procession, which took
place not long ago in one of the districts
of Paris, in which five hundred young
ladies walked dressed in white, and decorated with cockades of the national ribbon, leading by silken cords a number of
prisoners newly released from captivity,
and who, with their faces covered by long
flowing veils, were conducted to a church,
where they returned thanks for their deliverance.

Thus have the leaders of the revolution
engaged beauty as one of their auxiliaries,
justly concluding, that, to the gallantry
and sensibility of Frenchmen, no argument
would

would be found more efficacious than that of a pretty face.

I have just read a private letter from a little town about two leagues from Montauban, called Negre-Peliffe, where the inhabitants, on the day of the Federation, displayed a liberality of sentiment, which reflects honour, not only on themselves, but on the age in which we live. The national guard of this little town and its environs, were assembled to take the national oath. Half of the inhabitants being proteftants, and the other half Catholics, the Curé and the Proteftant Minifter ascended together one altar, which had been erected by the citizens, and administered the oath to their respective parishioners at the same moment, after which, Catholics and Protestants joined in singing Te Deum.

Surely religious worship was never performed more truly in the spirit of the Divine author of Chriftianity, whofe great precept is that of univerfal love! Surely

the

the incenſe of praiſe was never more likely to aſcend to heaven, than when the Catholics and Proteſtants of Negre-Peliſſe offered it together!

This amiable community, when their devotions were finiſhed, walked in proceſſion to a ſpot where fire-works had been prepared; and, it being conſidered as a mark of honour to light the fire-works, the office was reſerved for Monſ. le Curé, who, however, inſiſted on the participation of the proteſtant Miniſter in this diſtinction; upon which the Miniſter received a wax taper from the Curé, and with him led the proceſſion. The fire-works repreſented two trees. One, twiſted and diſtorted, was emblematical of ariſtocracy, and was ſoon entirely conſumed; when a tall ſtraight plant, figurative of patriotiſm, appeared to riſe from the aſhes of the former, and continued to burn with undiminiſhed ſplendour.

When we look back on the ignorance, the ſuperſtition, the barbarous perſecu-

tions

tions of Gothic times, is it not something to be thankful for, that we exist at this enlightened period, when such evils are no more; when particular tenets of religious belief are no longer imputed as crimes; when the human mind has made as many important discoveries in morality as in science, and liberality of sentiment is cultivated with as much success as arts and learning; when, in short, (and *you* are not one of those who will suspect that I am not all the while a good Englishwoman) when one can witness an event so sublime as the French revolution?

LETTER

L E T T E R IX.

YESTERDAY I received your letter, in which you accuse me of describing with too much enthusiasm the public rejoicings in France, and prophesy that I shall return to my own country a fierce republican. In answer to these accusations, I shall only observe, that it is very difficult, with common sensibility, to avoid sympathizing in general happiness. My love of the French revolution, is the natural result of this sympathy, and therefore my political creed is entirely an affair of the heart; for I have not been so absurd as to consult my head upon matters of which it is so incapable of judging. If I were at Rome, you would not be surprized to hear that I had visited, with the warmest reverence, every spot where any

relics

relics of her ancient grandeur could be traced; that I had flown to the capitol, that I had kiſſed the earth on which the Roman ſenate ſat in council: And can you then expect me to have ſeen the Federation at the Champ de Mars, and the National Aſſembly of France, with indiſſerence? Before you inſiſt that I ought to have done ſo, point out to me, in the page of Roman hiſtory, a ſpectacle more ſolemn, more affecting, than the Champ de Mars exhibited, or more magnanimous, more noble efforts in the cauſe of liberty than have been made by the National Aſſembly. Whether the new form of government, eſtabliſhing in France, be more or leſs perfect than our own,

" Who ſhall decide when doctors diſagree,
" And ſoundeſt caſuiſts doubt, like you and me?"

I fancy we had better leave the determination of this queſtion in the hands of poſterity. In the mean time, I wiſh that ſome of our political critics would ſpeak with leſs contempt, than they are apt to do,

of

of the new conſtitution of France, and no longer repeat after one another the trite remark, that the French have gone too far, becauſe they have gone farther than ourſelves; as if it were not poſſible that that degree of influence which is perfectly ſafe in the hand of the executive part of our government, might be dangerous, at this criſis, to the liberty of France. But be this as it may, it appears evident that the temple of Freedom which they are erecting, even if imperfect in ſome of its proportions, muſt be preferable to the old gloomy Gothic fabric which they have laid in ruins. And therefore, when I hear my good countrymen, who guard their own rights with ſuch unremitting vigilance, and who would rather part with life than liberty, ſpeak with contempt of the French for having imbibed the noble leſſon which England has taught, I cannot but ſuſpect that ſome mean jealouſy lurks beneath the ungenerous cenſure. I cannot but ſuſpect, that, while the fair and honourable

honourable traders of our commercial
country act with the most liberal spirit in
their ordinary dealings with other nations,
they wish to make a monopoly of liberty,
and are angry that France should claim
a share of that precious property; by
which, however, she may surely be enriched, without our being impoverished.
The French, on the contrary, seem to
have imbibed, with the principles of liberty, the strongest sentiments of respect
and friendship towards that people, whom
they gratefully acknowledge to have been
their masters in this science. They are,
to use their own phrase, * " devenus fous
des Anglois," and fondly imagine that
the applause they have received from a
society of philosophers in our country, is
the general voice of the nation.

Whether the new constitution be composed of durable materials or not, I leave
to politicians to determine; but it re-

* Become madly fond of the English.

quires

quiies no extraordinary fagacity to pro-
nounce, that the French will henceforth
be free. The love of liberty has per-
vaded all ranks of the people, who, if its
bleffings muft be purchafed with blood,
will not fhrink from paying the price:

" While ev'n the peafant boafts his rights to fcan,
" And learns to venerate himfelf as man."

The enthufiaftic fpirit of liberty difplays
itfelf, not merely on the days of folemn
ceremonies—occupies not only every ferious deliberation—but is mingled with
the gaiety of focial enjoyment. When
they converfe, liberty is the theme of dif-
courfe; when they dance, the figure of
the cotillon is adapted to a national
tune; and when they fing, it is but to
repeat a vow of fidelity to the conftitution, at which all who are prefent inftantly join in chorus, and fportively lift
up their hands in confirmation of this favourite fentiment.

In

In every street, you see children performing the military exercise, and carrying banners made of paper of the national colours, wearing grenadiers caps
of the same composition, and armed,
though not like Jack the Giant-killer,
with swords of sharpness.

Upon the whole, liberty appears in
France adorned with the freshness of
youth, and is loved with the ardour of
passion. In England she is seen in her
matron state, and, like other ladies at that
period, is beheld with sober veneration.

With respect to myself, I must acknowledge, that, in my admiration of the
revolution in France, I blend the feelings of private friendship with my sympathy in public blessings; since the old
constitution is connected in my mind with
the image of a friend confined in the
gloomy recesses of a dungeon, and pining
in hopeless captivity; while, with the new
constitution, I unite the soothing idea of

his

his return to prosperity, honours, and happiness.

This person is Monf. du F——, whose lady I am come to France to visit. They are friends with whom I wept in the day of their adversity, and with whom in their prosperity I have hastened to rejoice. Their history is most affecting; and, when I leave the hurry of Paris, to accompany them to their Chateau in Normandy, I will make you acquainted with incidents as pathetic as romance itself can furnish.   Adieu!

LETTER.

LETTER X.

WE have been driving at a furious rate, for several days paſt, through the city of Paris, which I think bears the ſame reſemblance to London (if you will allow me the indulgence of a ſimile) that the grand natural objects in a rude and barren country bear to the tame but regular beauties of a ſcene rich with cultivation. The ſtreets of Paris are narrow, dark, and dirty; but we are repaid for this by noble edifices, which powerfully intereſt the attention. The ſtreets of London are broad, airy, light, and elegant; but I need not tell you that they lead ſcarcely to any edifices at which foreigners do not look with contempt. London has, therefore, moſt of the beautiful, and Paris of the ſublime, according to Mr. Burke's definition

F.   nition

nition of thefe qualities; for I affure you a fenfation of terror is not wanting to the fublimity of Paris, while the coachman drives through the ftreets with the impetuofity of a Frenchman, and one expects every ftep the horfes take will be fatal to the foot paffengers, who are heard exclaiming, * " Que les rues de Paris font ariftocrates." By the way, *ariftocracie*, and *à la nation*, are become cant terms, which, as *Sterne* faid of *tant pis*, and *tant mieux*, may now be confidered as two of the great hinges in French converfation. Every thing tirefome or unpleafant, " c'eft une ariftocracie!" and every thing charming and agreeable is, " à la nation."

I have feen all the fine buildings at Paris, and fancy I fhould have admired the façade of the Louvre, the beautiful new church of St. Genevieve, and fome other edifices, even if I had not been told

* That the ftreets of Paris are ariftocrates

previoufly

previoufly, by a connoiffeur in thefe
matters, the precife degree of admiration
which it was proper to beftow on every
public building in Paris: but, having received fuch minute inftructions on this
fubject, I can form but an imperfect no-
tion of my own tafte for architecture.

At the requeft of Madame Brulart,
Monf. de Chartres fent orders for our admiffion to the Palais Royal, which is not
at prefent fhewn to the public. Of the
collection of pictures I am incapable of
faying any thing, and enough has been
already faid by thofe who underftand its
merits. Fine painting gives me confiderable pleafure, but has not the power
of calling forth my fenfibility like fine
poetry; and I am willing to believe that
the art I love is the moft perfect of the
two; and that it would have been impoffible for the pencil of Raphael to convey
all thofe ideas to the mind, and excite all

F 2 thofe

those emotions in the heart, which are awakened by the pen of Shakespeare.

I confess, the only picture in Paris which has cost me any tears, is that of La Valliere, in the convent of the Carmelites. She is represented in the habit of a Carmelite; all the former ornaments of her person lie scattered at her feet; and her eyes are cast up to Heaven with a look of the deepest anguish. While I gazed at her picture, I lamented that sensibility which led into the most fatal errors a mind that seems to have been formed for virtue, and which, even in the bosom of pleasure, bewailed its own weakness. How can one forbear regretting, that the capricious inconstant monarch, to whom she gave her heart, should have inspired a passion of which he was so unworthy ; a passion which appears to have been wholly unmixed with interest, vanity, or ambition? And how can one avoid pitying

ing

ing the desolate penitent, who, for so many years, in the dismal gloom of a convent, deplored her errors, and felt at once the bitterness of remorse, and the agony of disappointed love? while, probably,

"In every hymn she seem'd his voice to hear,
"And dropt with every bead, too soft a tear!"

If the figure of this beautiful Carmelite had not come across my imagination, I should have told you sooner, that the Palais Royal is a square, of which the Duc de Orleans's palace forms one side. You walk under piazzas round this square, which is surrounded with coffeehouses, and shops displaying a variety of ribbons, trinkets, and caricature prints, which are now as common at Paris as at London. The walks under the piazzas are crouded with people, and in the upper part of the square, tents are placed, where coffee, lemonade, ices, &c. are sold. Nothing is heard but the voice of

E 3 mirth;

mirth; nothing is feen but chearful
faces; and I have no doubt that the
Palais Royal is, upon the whole, one of
the merrieft fcenes under the fun. Indeed, what is moft ftriking to a ftranger
at Paris, is that general appearance of
gaiety, which it is eafy to perceive is not
affumed for the moment, but is the habit
of the mind, and which is, therefore,
fo exhilarating to a fpectator of any benevolence. It is this which gives fuch a
charm to every public place and walk in
Paris. Kenfington Gardens can boaft as
fine verdure, as majeftic trees, as noble
walks, and perhaps more beautiful women than the gardens of the Tuilleries,
but we fhall look in vain for that fpright-
ly animation, that everlafting chearful-
nefs, which render the Tuilleries fo enchanting.

We have juft returned from the Hopital des Invalides, a noble building, a-
dorned with fine paintings which record
the hiftory of fome celebrated faints,
                                    whofe

whofe exploits were recounted with in-
credible rapidity by the man who conducted us through the chapels, and who
feemed to think that nothing could be
more abfurd than our curiofity, after having heard thefe ftories from his lips, to
obferve how they were told by the pain-
ters.

As we paffed through the church, we
faw feveral old foldiers kneeling at the
confeffionals, with that folemn devotion
which feemed undifturbed by our intru-
fion, and fixed upon " the things that
are above."

A few days before the taking of the
Baftille, a croud of the Parifians affembled at the Hopital des Invalides, and
demanded arms of the old foldiers; who
anfwered, that they were the friends of
their fellow citizens, but durft not deliver up their arms without the appearance
of a conteft; and therefore defired that
the people would affemble before the
gates in greater numbers the next day,
when

when, after firing a little powder upon them, they would throw down their arms. The people accordingly returned the following day; and the invalids, after a faint shew of resistance, threw down their arms, which the citizens took up, embraced the old men, and then departed.

We stopped yesterday at La Maison de Ville, and went into a large apartment where the mayor and corporation assemble. The walls are hung round with pictures of Kings and Dukes, which I looked at with much less respect than at the chair on which Monf. Bailly fits. If his picture should ever be placed in this apartment, I fancy that, in the estimation of posterity, it will obtain precedency over all the Princes in the collection.

As we came out of La Maison de Ville, we were shewn, immediately opposite, the far-famed * lanterne, at

* The lamp-iron

which

which, for want of a gallows, the first victims of popular fury were sacrificed. I own that the fight of La Lanterne chilled the blood within my veins. At that moment, for the first time, I lamented the revolution; and, forgetting the imprudence, or the guilt, of those unfortunate men, could only reflect with horror on the dreadful expiation they had made I painted in my imagination the agonies of their families and friends, nor could I for a considerable time chafe these gloomy images from my thoughts.

It is for ever to be regretted, that so dark a shade of ferocious revenge was thrown acrofs the glories of the revolution. But, alas! where do the records of history point out a revolution unstained by some actions of barbarity? When do the passions of human nature rise to that pitch which produces great events, without wandering into some irregularities? If the French revolution should

E 5 cost

coſt no farther bloodſhed, it muſt be allowed, notwithſtanding a few ſhocking
inſtances of public vengeance, that the
liberty of twenty-four millions of people
will have been purchaſed at a far cheaper
rate than could ever have been expected from the former experience of the
world.

LETTER

LETTER XI.

WE are juft returned from Verfailles, where I could not help fancying I faw, in the back ground of that magnificent abode of a defpot, the gloomy dungeons of the Baftille, which ftill haunt my imagination, and prevented my being much dazzled by the fplendour of this fuperb palace.

We were fhewn the paffages through which the Queen efcaped from her own apartment to the King's. on the memorable night when the *Poiffardes* vifited Verfailles, and alfo the balcony at which fhe ftood with the Dauphin in her arms, when, after having remained a few hours concealed in fome fecret recefs of the palace, it was thought proper to comply with the defire of the croud, who repeatedly

peatedly demanded her presence. I could not help moralizing a little, on being told that the apartment to which this balcony belongs, is the very room in which Louis the Fourteenth died; little suspecting what a scene would, in the course of a few years, be acted on that spot.

All the bread which could be procured in the town of Versailles, was distributed among the *Poissardes*; who, with savage ferocity, held up their morsels of bread on their bloody pikes, towards the balcony where the Queen stood, crying, in a tone of defiance, * " Nous avons du pain!"

During the whole of the journey from Versailles to Paris, the Queen held the Dauphin in her arms, who had been previously taught to put his infant hands together, and attempt to soften the enraged multitude by repeating, † " Grace pour maman!"

* We now have bread   † Spare mama!

Monf.

Monf. de la Fayette prevented the whole Gardes du Corps from being maffacred at Verfailles, by calling to the incenfed people, * " Le Roi vous demande grace pour fes Gardes du Corps." The voice of Monf. de la Fayette was liftened to, and obeyed. The Gardes du Corps were fpared; with whom, before they fet out for Paris, the people exchanged clothes, giving them alfo national cockades; and as a farther protection from danger, part of the croud mounted on the horfes of the Gardes du Corps, each man taking an officer behind him. Before the King came out of La Maifon de Ville, Monf. de la Fayette appeared, and told the multitude, who had preferved an indignant filence the whole way from Verfailles to Paris, that the King had expreffed fentiments of the ftrongeft affection for his people, and had accepted the national cockade; and that he (Monf. de la Fayette) hoped,

* The King begs of you to fpare his body-guards.

when

when his Majesty came out of la Maison
de Ville, they would teftify their gratitude. In a few minutes the King appeared, and was received with the loud-
eft acclamations.

When the Queen was lately afked to
give her depofition on the attempt
which, it is faid, was made to affaffinate
her, by the *Poiffardes* at Verfailles, fhe
anfwered, with great prudence, " * Jai
tout vu, tout entendu, et tout oublié !"

The King is now extremely popular,
and the people fing in the ftreets to the
old tune of †" Vive Henri quatre! &c."
" Vive Louis feize!"

The Queen is, I am told, much altered late'y in her appearance, but fhe is
ftill a fine woman. Madame is a beautiful girl; and the Dauphin, who is
about feven years of age, is the idol of
the people. They expect that he will be

* I faw every thing, heard every thing, and have
forgot every-thing.

† Long live Henry the fourth. Long live Lewis
the Sixteenth.

educated

educated in the principles of the new constitution, and will be taught to consider himself less a king than a citizen. He appears to be a sweet engaging child, and I have just heard one of his sayings repeated. He has a collection of animals, which he feeds with his own hand. A few days ago, an ungrateful rabbit, who was his first favourite, bit his finger when he was giving him food. The Prince, while smarting with the pain, called out to his * petit lapin, "Tu ès Aristocrate." One of the attendants enquired, "Eh! Monseigneur, qu'est-ce que c'est qu'un Aristocrate." "Ce font ceux," answered the Prince, "qui font de la peine à Papa."

The King lately called the Queen, en badinage, Madame Capet; to which she retorted very readily, by giving his Ma-

* Little rabbit, Thou art an Aristocrate.— And pray, my Lord, what is an Aristocrate?—Those who make my papa uneasy.

jesty

jefty the appellation of " Monſieur * Capot."

When Les gardes Francoiſes laid down
their arms at Verſailles, their officers endeavoured to perſuade them to take them
up... An officer of my acquaintance told
me, that he ſaid to his ſoldiers, † " Mes
enfans, vous allez donc me quitter, vous
ne m'aimez plus ?" " Mon officier," they
anſwered, " nous vous aimons tous, ſi il
s'agit d'aller contre nos ennemis, nous
ſommes tous prets à vous ſuivre, mais
nous ne tirerons jamais contre nos com-
patriotes " Since that period, whenever
any of les gardes Francoiſes appear; they
are followed by the acclamations of the

* Capot is the French term at picquet, when the
game is loſt:

† My friends, you are going then to forſake me ;
I poſſeſs none of your affection—Captain, they anſwered, we all love you ; and, if you will lead us
againſt our enemies, we are all ready to follow you :
but we will never fire at our fellow citizens.

people

people, and "* Vive les Gardes Fran-coises!" resounds from every quarter.

While we were sitting, after dinner, at the inn at Versailles, the door was sud-denly opened, and a Franciscan friar en-tered the room. He had so strong a re-semblance to Sterne's monk, that I am persuaded he must be a descendant of the same family. We could not, like Sterne, bestow immortality; but we gave some alms: and the venerable old monk, after thanking us with affecting simplici-ty, added, spreading out his hands with a flow and solemn movement, † " Que la paix soit avec vous," and then departed. I have been frequently put in mind of Sterne since my arrival in France; and the first post-boy I saw in jack-boots, ap-peared to me a very classical figure, by recalling the idea of La Fleur mounted on his bidet.

* Long live the French guards.
† Peace be with you.

LETTER

LETTER XII.

WE have been at all the Theatres, and I am charmed with the comic actors. The tragic performers afforded me much lefs pleafure. Before we can admire Madame Veftris, the firft tragic actrefs of Paris, we muft have loft the impreffion (a thing impoffible) of Mrs. Siddons's performance; who, inftead of "tearing a paffion to rage," like Madame Veftris, only tears the hearts of the audience with fympathy.

Moft of the pieces we have feen at the French theatres have been little comedies relative to the circumftances of the times, and, on that account, pieferred, in this moment of enthufiafm, to all the wit of Moliere. Thefe little pieces might perhaps read coldly enough in your

your study, but have a moft charming effect with an accompanyment of applaufe from fome hundreds of the national guards, the real actors in the fcenes reprefented. Between the acts national fongs are played, in which the whole audience join in chorus. There is one air, in particular, which is fo univerfal a favourite, that it is called "Le Carrillon National:" the burden of the fong is * " C'a ira." It is fung not only at every theatre, and in every ftreet of Paris, but in every town and village of France, by man, woman, and child. " C'a ira" is every where the fignal of pleafure, the beloved found which animates every bofom with delight, and of which every ear is enamoured. And I have heard the moft ferious political converfations end by a fportive affurance, in allufion to this fong, que " C'a ira!"

* It will go on.

Giornowiche

Giornowiche, the celebrated player on the violin, who was so much the fashion laft winter at London, I am told, sometimes amufed himfelf at Paris, by getting up into one of the trees of the Palais Royal, after it was dark, and calling forth tones from his violin, fit to " take the prifon'd foul, and lap it in Elyfium." He has frequently detained fome thoufands of people half the night in the Palais Royal, who, before they difcovered the performer, ufed to call out in rapture, " Bravo, bravo; * c'eft mieux que Giornowiche."

I am juft returned from feeing the Gobelin tapeftry, which appears the work of magic. It gave me pleafure to fee two pictures of Henry the Fourth. In one, he is placed at fupper with the milker's family; and in the other, he is embracing Sully, who is brought forward on a couch, after having been wounded

---

* This is better than Giornowiche.

in

in battle. Nothing has afforded me
more delight, since I came to France,
than the honours which are paid to my
favourite hero, Henry the Fourth,
whom I prefer to all the Alexanders and
Frederics that ever existed. They may
be terribly sublime, if you will, and
have great claims to my admiration; but
as for my love, all that portion of it
which I bestow on heroes, is already in
Henry's possession.

Little statues of Henry the Fourth and
Sully are very common. Sully is represented kneeling at the feet of this amiable
Prince, who holds out his hand to him;
and on the base of the statue, are written
the words which Sully records in his Memoirs: *" Mais levez vous, levez vous
donc, Sully, on croiroit que je vous par-
donne."

While the statue of Henry the Fourth,
on the Pont Neuf, is illuminated and de-

* But rise, pray rise, Sully; they will believe
I am forgiving you.

corated

corated with national ribbon, that of
Louis the Fourteenth, in the Place Vic-
toire, is ftripped of its former oftentati-
ous ornaments; the nations, which were
reprefented enchained at his feet, having
been removed fince the revolution. The
figure of Fame is, however, ftill left ho-
vering behind the ftatue of the King,
with a crown of laurel in her hand,
which it is generally fuppofed, fhe is going to place upon his head. But I have
heard of a French wit, who enquired
whether it was really her intention to
place the laurel on his Majefty's head, or
whether fhe had juft taken it off.

In our ride this morning, we ftopped
at the Place Royal, where I was diverted
by reading, on the front of a little fhop
under the piazzas, thefe words: " Robelin, * ecrivain. — Memoires et letters
écrites à jufte prix, à la nation." I am

* Writer.—Memoirs and letters written at a mo-
derate price, for the Nation.

told,

told, that Monf. Robelin is in very flou-
rifhing bufinefs; and perhaps I might
have had recourfe to him for affiftance in
my correfpondence with you, if I did
not leave Paris to-morrow. You fhall
hear from me from Rouen.

LETTER

LETTER XIII.

WE had a moſt agreeable journey from Paris to Rouen, travelling a hundred miles along the borders of the Seine, through a beautiful country, richly wooded, and finely diverſified by hill and valley. We paſſed ſeveral magnificent chateaus, and ſaw many a ſpire belonging to Gothic edifices, which, it would ſeem, were built of ſuch laſting materials, with the moral purpoſe of leading the mind to reflect cn the comparatively ſhort duration of human life. Frequently an old venerable croſs, placed at the ſide of the road by the piety of remote ages, and never paſſed by Roman Catholics without ſome mark of reſpect, throws a kind of religious ſanctity over the landſcape.

We

We stopped to look at the immense machine which conveys water to Versailles and Marly. The water is raised, by means of this machine, sixty feet, and is carried the distance of five hundred. I never heard a sound which filled my mind with more horror than the noise occasioned by the movements of this tremendous machine; while, at the same time, the vast chasms, where the water foams with angry violence, make the brain giddy, and I was glad to leave these images of terror.

Part of our journey was performed by moon-light, which slept most sweetly upon the bank, and spread over the landscape those softned graces which I will not attempt to describe, lest my pen should stray into rhyme.

We passed the chateau of Rosni, a noble domain given to Sully by Henry the Fourth; a testimony of that friendship which reflects equal honour on the King and the Minister.

F   About

About three leagues from Rouen stands a convent, of which Abelard was for some time the superior. It is still inhabited by a few monks, and is called Le Couvent de deux Amans. Had it been the monastery of the Paraclete, the residence of Eloisa, I should have hastened to visit the spot,

> " Where, o'er the twilight groves and dusky caves,
> " Long founding isles, and intermingled graves,
> " Black Melancholy sits, and round her throws
> " A death-like silence, and a dread repose;
> " Her gloomy presence saddens all the scene,
> " Shades ev'ry flow'r, and darkens ev'ry green,
> " Deepens the murmur of the falling floods,
> " And breathes a browner horror on the woods "

If it were not very difficult to be angry with such a poet as Pope, particularly after having just transcribed these exquisite lines, I should be so when I recollect how clearly Mr. Berington shows, in his History of Abelard and Eloisa, the cruel injustice done by Pope to the sentiments of Eloisa, who is too often made to speak a very different language in the poem, from that of her genuine letters.

On

On our way to Rouen we flept at Gallon, a town about five leagues diftant. Our inn was clofe to the caftle, which formerly belonged to the Archbifhop of Rouen, and which is now the property of the nation. The caftle is a venerable gothic building, with a fine orangery, and parks which extend feveral leagues. The Archbifhop, who is the Cardinal de la Rochefoucault, brother to that diftinguifhed patriot the ci devant Duc de la Rochefoucault, has loft a very confiderable revenue fince the revolution. He had an immenfe train of fervants, whom it is faid he difmiffed, upon the diminution of his income, with all poffible gentlenefs, giving horfes to one, a carriage to another, and endeavouring to beftow on all fome little alleviation of the pain they felt at quitting fo good a mafter. It is impoffible not to regret that the property of the Cardinal de la Rochefoucault is diminifhed, by whom it was only employed in difpenfing happinefs.

F 2 After

After visiting the castle, I returned somewhat in mournful mood to the inn, where there was nothing calculated to convey one chearful idea. The cieling of our apartment was crossed with old bare beams; the tapestry, with which the room was hung, displayed, like the dress of Otway's old woman, " variety of wretchedness;" the canopied beds were of coarse dirty stuff; two pictures, in tawdry gilt frames, slandered the sweet countenances of the Dauphin and Madame; and the floor was paved with brick. In short, one can scarcely imagine a scene more remote from England, in accommodation and comfort, than the country inns of France : yet, in this habitation, where an Englishman would have been inclined to hang himself, was my rest disturbed half the night by the merry songs which were sung in an adjoining apartment, as gloomy as my own. But those local circumstances,
which

which affect Englifh nerves, never dif-
turb the peace of that happy people, by
whom, whether engaged in taking the
Baftille, or fitting with their friends after
fupper, * tout fe fait en chantant.

* Every thing is done finging.

F 3 LETTER

LETTER XIV.

ROUEN is one of the largest and most commercial towns of France. It is situated on the banks of the Seine, has a fine quay, and a singular bridge, of barges placed close together, with planks fixed upon them: the bridge rises and sinks with the tide, and opens for vessels to pass.

The streets of Rouen are so narrow, dark, and frightful, that, to borrow an expression from Madame Sevigné, * " elles abusent de la permission qu'ont les rues Françoises d'être laides." There are many figures of Saints to be seen from these ugly streets, placed in little niches in the walls   The Virgin Mary is seated

* " They abuse the permission the French streets have of being ugly."

in

in one of thefe niches, with the infant in her arms ; and in the neighbourhood is St. Anne, who has the credit of having taught the Virgin to read. Every night the general darkneſs of the town is a little difpelled by the lamps which the people place in the niches, * " pour ec-lairer les Saints "

Rouen is furrounded by fine boule-vards, that form very beautiful walks. On the top of the hill of Ste Catharine, which overlooks the town, are the ruins of a fort called St. Michell, from which Henry the Fourth befieged Rouen. I love to be put in mind of Henry the Fourth, and am therefore very well plea-fed, that when ever I go to walk, I can fix my eyes on the hill of Ste Catharine.

I always feel a little afhamed of my country, when I pafs the fpot where the Maid of Orleans was executed, and on

* " To light the Saints."

which

which her ſtatue ſtands, a monument of our diſgrace. The aſhes of her perſecutor, John Duke of Bedford, repoſe at no great diſtance, within a tomb of black marble, in the cathedral, which was built by the Engliſh. One cannot feel much reſpect for the judgment of our anceſtors, in chuſing, of all places under the ſun the cathedral of Rouen for the tomb of him whoſe name is tranſmitted to us with the epithet of the *good* Duke of Bedford: for you have ſcarcely left the cathedral, before the ſtatue of Jeane d'Arc ſtares you in the face, and ſeems to caſt a moſt formidable ſhade over the *good* Duke's virtues.

The cathedral is a very magnificent edifice, and the great bell is ten feet high, and weighs thirty-ſix thouſand pounds. But in France it is not what is *antient*, but what is *modern*, that moſt powerfully engages attention. Nothing in this fine old cathedral intereſted me ſo much as

the

the confecrated banner, which fince the
Federation, has been placed over the altar, and on which is infcribed, " * Vivons libres, ou mourons !" I hope every
Frenchman, who enters the cathedral of
Rouen, while he reads the infcription on
this confecrated banner, repeats from the
bottom of his foul, † " Vivons libres ou
mourons!" But the French will, I truft,
efcape the horrors of civil war, notwithftanding the gloomy forebodings of the
enemies of the new conftitution.

A people juft delivered from the yoke
of oppreffion, will furely have little incli-
nation to refume their fhackles; to re-
build the dungeons they have fo lately demolifhed; to clofe again thofe gloomy
monaftic gates which are now thrown
open; to exchange their new courts of
judicature, founded on the bafis of juftice
and humanity, for the caprice of power;

* Let us live free, or die!
† Let us live free, or die!

and

and the dark iniquity of letters de cachét; to quench the fair star of liberty, which has arisen on their hemisphere, and suffer themselves to be once more guided by the meteor of despotism.

A very considerable number, even among the nobility of France, have had the virtue to support the cause of freedom; and, forgetting the little considerations of vanity, which have some importance in the ordinary course of human affairs, but which are lost and annihilated when the mind is animated by any great sentiment, they have chosen to become the benefactors rather than the oppressors of their country; the citizens of a free state, instead of the slaves of a despotic monarch. They will no longer bear arms to gratify the ambition, or the caprice of a minister; they will no longer exert that impetuous and gallant spirit, for which they have ever been distinguished, in any cause unworthy of its efforts. The fire

fire of valour, which they have too often
employed for the purposes of destruction,
will henceforth be directed to more generous ends. They will chuse another
path to renown. Instead of attempting
to take the citadel of glory by storm, they
will prefer the fame of an honourable defence, and, renouncing the sanguinary
laurel, strive, with more exalted enthusiasm, to obtain the civic wreath. Yes,
the French nation will inviolably guard,
will transmit to posterity the sacred
rights of freedom. Future ages will ce-
lebrate, with grateful commemoration,
the fourteenth of july; and strangers,
when they visit France, will hasten with
impatience to the Champ de Mars, filled
with that enthusiasm which is awakened
by the view of a place where any great
scene has been acted. I think I hear
them exclaim, " Here the Federation was
held ! here an assembled nation devoted
themselves to freedom !" I fancy I see
them pointing out the spot on which the

altar

altar of the country ſtood. I ſee them eagerly ſearching for the place where they have heard it recorded, that the National Aſſembly were ſeated! I think of theſe things, and then repeat to myſelf with tranſport, " *I*, was a ſpectator of the Federation !"

But theſe meditations have led me to travel through the ſpace of ſo many centuries, that it is really difficult to get back again to the preſent times. Did you expect that I ſhould ever dip my pen in politics, who uſed to take ſo ſmall an intereſt in public affairs, that I recollect a gentleman of my acquaintance ſurprized me not a little, by informing me of the war between the Turks and the Ruſſians, at a time when all the people of Europe, exept myſelf, had been two years in poſſeſſion of this intelligence?

If, however, my love of the French revolution requires an apology, you ſhall receive one in a very ſhort time; for I

am

am going to Monſ. du F——'s chateau, and will ſend you from thence the hiſtory of his misfortunes. They were the inflictions of tyranny, and you will rejoice with me that tyranny is no more.

Before I cloſe my letter, I ſhall mention a ſingular privilege of the church of Rouen, which is the power of ſetting free a murderer every year on the day of Aſcenſion. It ſeems that in the time of King Dagobert, who reigned in the ſixth century, a horrible and unrelenting dragon deſolated the country, ſparing neither man nor beaſt. St. Romain, who was then biſhop of Rouen, aſked for two criminals to aſſiſt him in an enterprize he had the courage to meditate againſt the dragon; and with theſe aides de camp he ſallied forth, killed the monſter, and delivered the country. In conſequence of this miracle, Dagobert gave the ſucceſſors of St. Romain the privilege of ſetting a murderer free every year on Aſcenſion-day.

day. The bones of St. Romain are carried by the criminal in a gilt box through the streets: the figure of a hideous animal reprefenting the dragon, though it is fufpected of flandering his countenance, accompanies thefe venerable bones, and has generally a young living wolf placed in its maw, except when it is * jour maigre, and then the dragon is provided with a large fifh. The counfellors of the parliament, dreffed in their fcarlet robes, attend this proceffion to a church, where high mafs is faid; and, thefe ceremonies being performed, the criminal is fet at liberty. But it is only when there are fome ftrong alleviating circumftances in the cafe of the offender, that he is fuffered in this manner to evade the punifhment of his crimes.

Yefterday, in a little town called Sotte Ville, joined to Rouen by the bridge, a political difpute arofe between the Curé and his parifhioners. The enraged Curé

* Faft-day.

exclaimed,

exclaimed, * " Vous êtes une affemblée d'anes."   To which one of the parifhioners anfwered, with great calmnefs, +" Oui Monf. le Curé, et vous en êtes le pafteur."

* You are an affembly of affes.
+ Yes, Sir, and you are our preacher.

LETTER

L E T T E R XV.

I HEARD * La meſſe militaire, on Sunday laſt, at a church where all the national guard of Rouen attended. The ſervice began with the loudeſt thunder of drums and trumpets, and ſeemed more like a ſignal for battle than for devotion; but the muſic ſoon ſoftened into the moſt ſoothing ſounds, which flowed from the organ, clarinets, flutes, and hautboys; the prieſts chanted, and the people made reſponſes. The wax tapers were lighted, holy water was ſprinkled on the ground, incenſe was burnt at the altar, and the elevation of the hoſt was announced by the ſound of the drum; upon which the people knelt down, and the prieſt proſtrated his face towards the earth. There

* The military maſs.

is

is something affecting in the pomp and
solemnity of these ceremonies. Indeed,
the Roman Catholic worship, though a
sad stumbling-block to reason, is striking
to the imagination. I have more than
once heard the service for the dead performed, and never can hear it without
emotion; without feeling that in those
melancholy separations, which bury every
hope of the survivor in the relentless
grave, the heart that can delude itself with
the belief, that its prayers may avail any
thing to the departed object of its affections, must find consolation in thus uniting a tribute of tenderness, with the performance of a religious duty.

We have been at several convents at
Rouen. The first to which we went was a
convent of benedictine nuns. When we
had entered the gates we rang a bell, and
a servant appeared, and desired us to go
up stairs to the parloir. We opened a
wrong door, and found, in a room grated
across

across the middle with iron bars, a young
man sitting on one side of the grate, and
a young nun on the other.   I could not
help thinking that the heart of this young
man was placed in a perilous situation;
for where can a young woman appear so
interesting, as when seen within that
gloomy barrier, which death alone can
remove?   What is there, in all the osten-
tation of female dress, so likely to affect a
man of sensibility, as that dismal habit
which seems so much at variance with
youth and beauty, and is worn as the melancholy symbol of an eternal renuncia-
tion of the world and all its pleasures?
We made an apology to the nun for our
intrusion, and she directed us to another
apartment, where, a few minutes after we
had seated ourselves on one side of the
grate, La Depositaire entered on the
other, and told us that the Abbess, whom
we had desired to see, was not yet risen
from dinner, and La Depositaire hoped
                                            we

we would wait a little. * " Parceque,"
said she, " Madame l'Abbesse etoit obli-
gée hier de se lever de table de bonne he-
ure, et elle se trouvoit une peu incom-
modée." You must observe that the
Abbesse dined at three o'clock, and it was
now past six. At length this lady, who
was so fond of long dinners, appeared.
She is a woman of fifty, but is still hand-
some; has a frank agreeable countenance,
fine eyes, and had put on her veil in a
very becoming manner. We wished to
be admitted to the interior part of the
convent, and with this view a French
gentleman, who was of our party, †se se
mit à conter des histoires à Madame
l'Abbesse."

He told her that my sister and I, though
English women, were catholics, and wished

* Because, said she, the Abbess was obliged to rise
from table very soon yesterday, and found herself a
little indisposed.

† Told a great many fables to the Abbess.

to

to be received into the convent, and even,
if it had been poffible, to take the vows.
The Abbefs enquired if he was quite fure
of our being catholics; upon which the
gentleman, a little puzzled what to anfwer, infinuated that Monf. du F—— had
probably the merit of our converfion.
" But I have heard," faid the Abbefs,
" from Madame ——, that Monf. du
F—— has become a proteftant himfelf."
Monf. du F——, who is truth itfelf,
avowed his principles without hefitation;
while the Abbefs, turning to La Depofitaire, exclaimed, * " Mais comme Monf.
eft aimable! quel beaux fentiments ! Ah
Monf. vous êtes trop bon pour que Dieu
vous laiffe dans l'erreur." " St. Auguftin," continued fhe, " had once fome
doubts; I hope you will be a fecond St.
Auguftin: myfelf, and all my communi-

---

* How amiable he is! what noble fentiments !
Ah, Sir, you are too good for God to leave you in
error.

ty,

ty, will pray for your converfion." La
Depofitaire, who was a tall thin old woman, with a fharp malignant countenance,
added, cafting a look on Monf. du F——,
full of the contempt of fuperior knowledge, "It is not furprizing that a young
man, after pafling feveral years in England, that country of heretics, fhould find
his faith fomewhat fhaken; but he only
wants to be enlightned by Monf. le Curé
de ——, who will immediately diffipate
all his doubts."

From the Convent of the Benedictines
we went to that of the Carmelites, where
religion, which was meant to be a fourcc
of happinefs in this world, as well as in
the next, wears an afpect of the moft
gloomy horror. When we entered the
convent, it feemed the refidence of filence
and folitude: no voice was heard, no human creature appeared; and when we
rang the bell, a perfon, whom we could
not fee, enquired, through a hole in the
wall,

wall, what we wanted. On being informed that we wished to speak to the Superieure, putting her hand through the
hole, she gave us a key, and desired us
to unlock the door of the parloir. This
we accordingly did; and in a few minutés
the Superieure came to a thick double
grate, with a curtain drawn at the inside,
to prevent the possibility of being seen.
Our French gentleman again talked of
our desire to enter the convent, and begged to know the rules   A hollow voice
answered, that the Carmelites rose at four
in the morning in summer, and five in
the winter:—" Obedient slumbers, that
can wake and weep!"—That they slept
in their coffins, upon straw, and every
morning dug a shovel-full of earth for
their graves; that they walked to their
devotional exercifes upon their knees;
that when any of their friends visited them,
if they spoke, they were not suffered to be
seen, or if they were seen, they were not
                                        suffered

ſuffered to ſpeak; that with them it was * toujours maigre, and they only taſted food twice a day.

Our Frenchman ſaid, "† Il faut Madame que ces demoiſelles reflechiſſent, ſi cela leur convient." The poor Carmelite agreed that the matter required ſome reflection, and we departed.

As we returned home meditating on the lot of a Carmelite, we met in the ſtreet three nuns walking in the habit of their order. Upon enquiry, we were told that they had been forced by their parents to take the veil, and, ſince the decree of the National Aſſembly giving them liberty, they had obtained permiſſion to pay a viſit for three months to ſome friends who ſympathized in their unhappineſs, and were now on their journey.

The monks and nuns muſt in a ſhort

---

* Always a faſt.

† Theſe young ladies, Madam, muſt conſider whether theſe regulations will ſuit them.

time

time decide whether they will finally leave their cloifters or not; and the religious houfes which are vacated will be fold. In the department of Rouen a calculation has been made, that, after paying every monk feven hundred, and every nun five hundred livres a year, out of the revenues of the religious houfes, the department will gain fixty thoufand livres a year. The monks and nuns above fixty years of age, who chufe to leave their convents, will be allowed an annual penfion of nine hundred livres.

A letter was read in the National Affembly, a few days ago, from a prieft, intreating that the clergy might have permiffion to marry; a privilege which it is thought the Affembly will foon authorize.   * " On a bouleverfé tout," faid an old Curé, a fierce Ariftocrate, with whom I was in company, † " Et meme on veut

* They have overturned every thing.

† And would even carry the profanation fo far as to fuffer the priefts to marry.

porter

porter la profanation ſi loin que de marier les pretres." It is conjectured, however, that the younger part of the clergy think of this meaſure with leſs horror than the old Curé.

We arrived laſt night at Monſ. du F——'s chateau, without having viſited, during our ſtay at Rouen, the tomb of William the Conqueror, who is buried at Caen, a town twelve leagues diſtant. But I have been too lately at the Champ de Mars, to travel twelve leagues in order to ſee the tomb of a tyrant.

Upon Monſ. du F——'s arrival at the chateau, all his tenants, with their wives and daughters, came to pay their reſpects to Mon Seigneur, and were addreſſed by Monſ. and Madame with thoſe endearing epithets which give ſuch a charm to the French language, and are ſo much more rejoicing to the heart than our formal appellations. Here a peaſant girl is termed, by the lady of the chateau,

G

"Ma

* " Ma bonne amie, Ma petite, Mon enfant;" while thofe pretty monofyllables
† tu, ta, &c. ufed only to the neareſt re-
lations, and to ſervants, imprefs the mind
with the idea of that affectionate famili-
arity, which ſo gracefully ſoftens the diftance of fituation, and excites in the de-
pendant, not preſumption, but gratitude.
‡ " Et comment te porte tu, La Voie ?"
ſaid Monf. du F——— to one of his farmers. " § Affez bien Mon Seigneur,"
replied he; " mais j'eus la fievre a Pacque,
à votre ſervice."

* My good friend, My little girl, My child.

† 'Thou, thy, &c

‡ And how do you do, La Voie ?

§ Pretty well, my Lord; but I had a fover laſt
Eaſter, at your ſervice.

LETTER

LETTER XVI.

I Embrace the firſt hours of leiſure, which I have found ſince my arrival at the chateau, to ſend you the hiſtory of my friends.

Antoine Auguſtin Thomás du F——, eldeſt ſon of the Baron du F——, Counſellor of the Parliament of Normandy; was born on the fifteenth of July, 1750. His early years were embittered by the ſeverity of his father, who was of a diſpoſition that preferred the exerciſe of domeſtic tyranny to the bleſſings of ſocial happineſs, and choſe rather to be dreaded than beloved. The endearing name of father conveyed no tranſport to *his* heart, which, being wrapt up in ſtern inſenſibility, was cold even to the common feelings of nature.

G 2 The

The Baron's aufterity was not indeed confined to his fon, but extended to all his dependants. Formed by nature for the fupport of the antient government of France, he maintained his ariftocratic rights with unrelenting feverity, ruled his feudal tenures with a rod of iron, and confidered the lower order of people as a fet of beings whofe exiftence was tolerated merely for the ufe of the nobility. The poor, he believed, were only born for fuffering ; and he determined, as far as in him lay, not to deprive them of their natural inheritance. On the whole, if it were the great purpofe of human life to be hated, perhaps no perfon ever attained that end more completely than the Baron Du F——.

His fon difcovered early a tafte for literature, and received an education fuitable to his rank and fortune. As he advanced in life, the treatment he experienced from his father became more and

more

more intolerable to him, as, far from inheriting the fame character, he poffeffed the moft amiable difpofitions, and the moft feeling heart

His mother, feeble alike in mind and body, fubmitted with the helplefsnefs, and almoft with the thoughtlefsnefs of a child, to the imperious will of her hufband. Their family was increafed by two more fons, and two daughters; but thefe children, being feveral years younger than Monf. Du F——, were not of an age to afford him the confolations of friendfhip; and the young man would have found his fituation intolerable, but for the fympathy of a perfon, in whofe fociety every evil was forgotten.

This perfon, his attachment to whom has tinctured the colour of his life, was the youngeft of eight children, of a refpectable family of Bourgeois at Rouen. There is great reafon to believe that her father was defcended from the younger branch of a noble family of the fame name, and bearing the fame arms. But, unhappily, fome links were wanting in this chain of honourable parentage. The claim to nobility could not be traced to the entire fatisfaction of the Baron ; who, though he would have difpenfed with any moral qualities in favour of rank, confidered obfcure birth as a radical ftain, which could not be wiped off by all the virtues under heaven. He locked upon marriage as merely a convention of intereft, and children as a property, of which it was reafonable for parents to make the moft in their power.

The father of Mad^{felle} Monique C—— was a farmer, and died three months before the birth of this child ; who, with feven other children, was educated with the utmoft care by their mother, a woman of fenfe and virtue, beloved by all to whom fhe was known. It feemed as if this refpectable woman had, after the

death

death of her hufband, only fupported life for the fake of her infant family, from whom fhe was fnatched by death, the moment her maternal cares became no longer neceffary; her youngeft daughter, Monique, having, at this period, juft attained her twentieth year. Upon the death of her mother, Monique went to live with an aunt, with whom fhe remained only a very fhort time, being invited by Madame du F——, to whom fhe was well known, to come and live with her as an humble companion, to read to her when fhe was difpofed to liften, and to enliven the fullen grandeur of the chateau, by her animating vivacity.

This young perfon had cultivated her excellent underftanding by reading, and her heart ftood in no need of cultivation. Monf. Du F——found in the charms of her converfation, and in the fympathy of her friendfhip, the moft foothing confolation under the rigor of parental tyranny. Living feveral years beneath the fame

roof, he had conftant opportunities of ob-
ferving her difpofition and character;
and the paffion with which fhe at length
infpired him, was founded on the lafting
bafis of efteem.

If it was ever pardonable to deviate
from that law, in the code of intereft and
etiquette, which forbids the heart to liften to its beft emotions; **which, ftifling
every generous fentiment of pure difinte-
refted attachment, facrifices love at the
fhrine of avarice or ambition; the virtues of Monique were fuch as might excufe this deviation. Yes, the character,**
the conduct of this amiable perfon, have
nobly juftified her lover's choice. How
long might he have vainly fought, in the
higheft claffes of fociety, a mind fo elevated above the common mafs!—a mind
that, endowed with the moft exquifite fenfibility, has had fufficient firmnefs to fuftain, with a calm and equal fpirit, every
tranfition of fortune; the moft fevere
trials

trials of adverfity, and perhaps what is ftill more difficult to bear, the trial of high profperity.

Monf. Du F—— had been taught, by his early misfortunes, that domeftic happinefs was the firft good of life. He had already found, by experience, the infufficiency of rank and fortune to confer enjoyment; and he determined to feek it in the bofom of conjugal felicity. He determined to pafs his life with her whofe fociety now feemed effential not only to his happinefs, but to his very exiftence.

At the folemn hour of midnight, the young couple went to a church, where they were met by a prieft whom Monf. Du F—— had made the confident of his attachment, and by whom the marriage ceremony was performed.

Some time after, when the fituation of his wife obliged Monf. Du F—— to acknowledge their marriage to his mother, fhe affured her fon that fhe would willingly confent to receive his wife as her daughter,

daughter, but for the dread of his father's resentment. Madame Du F——, with tears of regret, parted with Monique, whom she placed under the protection of her brothers: they conducted her to Caen, where she was soon after delivered of a son.

The Baron Du F——— was absent while these things were passing; he had been suspected of being the author of a pamphlet written against the princes of the blood, and an order was issued to seize his papers, and conduct him to the Bastille; but he found means to escape into Holland, where he remained nearly two years. Having made his peace with the ministry, he prepared to come home; but before he returned, Monf. Du F—— received intelligence that his father, irritated almost to madness by the information of his marriage, was making application for a lettre de cachet, in order to confine his daughter-in-law for the rest of her life; and had also obtained power to

have

have his son seized and imprisoned. Upon this Monf. Du F——— and his wife fled with precipitation to Geneva, leaving their infant at nurse near Caen. The Genevois seemed to think that the unfortunate situation of these strangers, gave them a claim to all the offices of friendship. After an interval of many years, I have never heard Monf. or Madame Du F——— recall the kindness they received from that amiable people, without tears of tenderness and gratitude.

Meanwhile the Baron, having discovered the place of his son's retreat, obtained, in the name of the King, permission from the cantons of Berne and Friburg to arrest them at Laufanne, where they had retired for some months. The wife of Le Seigneur Baillif secretly gave the young people notice of this design, and on the thirtieth of January, 1775, they had just time to make their escape, with only a few livres in their pockets, and the cloaths in which they were dressed.

Monf.

Monf. Du F——, upon his firft going to Switzerland, had lent thirty louis to a friend in diftrefs. He now, in this moment of neceffity, defired to be repaid, and was promifed the money within a month: mean time, he and his wife wandered from town to town, without finding any place where they could remain in fecurity. They had fpent all their fmall ftock of money, and were almoft without clothes: but at the expiration of the appointed time, the thirty louis were paid, and with this fund Monf. and Madame Du F—— determined to take fhelter in the only country which could afford them a fafe afylum from perfecution, and immediately fet off for England, travelling through Germany, and part of Holland, to avoid paffing through France.

They embarked at Roterdam, and, after a long and gloomy paffage, arrived late at night at London. A young man, who was their fellow paffenger, had the charity to procure them a lodging in a
garret,

garret, and directed them where to pur-
chafe a few ready-made clothes. When
they had remained in this lodging the
time neceffary for becoming parifhioners,
their bans were publifhed in the church of
St. Anne, Weftminfter, where they were
married by the Curate of the parifh.
They then went to the chapel of the
French Ambaffador, and were again married by his Chaplain; after which Monf.
Du F—— told me, * Les deux epoux
vinrent faire maigre chaire à leur petite
chambre."

Monf. Du F—— endeavoured to obtain a fituation at a fchool, to teach the
French language; but before fuch a fituation could be found, his wife was delivered of a girl. Not having fufficient
money to hire a nurfe, he attended her
himfelf. At this period they endured all
the horrors of abfolute want. Unknown
and unpitied, without help or fupport, in

* The new married couple kept a faft in their
little apartment.

a for-

a foreign country, and in the depth of a
fevere winter, they almoft perifhed with
cold and hunger. The unhappy mother
lay ftretched upon the fame bed with her
new-born infant, who in vain implored
her fuccour, want of food having dried
up that fource of nourifhment. The woman, at whofe houfe they lodged, and
whom they had for fome weeks been unable to pay, after many threatenings, at
lenth told them that they muft depart the
uext morning. Madame Du F——was
at this time fcarcely able to walk acrofs
her chamber, and the ground was covered
with fnow. They had already exhaufted
every refource ; they had fold their
watches, their clothes, to fatisfy the crav-
ings of hunger ; every mode of relief was
fled——every avenue of hope was clofed——
and they determined to go with their infant to the fuburbs of the town, and there
featedon a ftone, wait with patience for
the deliverance of death. With what anguifh did this unfortunate couple pre-
                                        pare

pare to leave their laſt miſerable retreat! With how many bitter tears did they bathe that wretched infant, whom they could no longer ſave from periſhing!

Oh, my dear, my ever beloved friends! when I recollect that I am not at this moment indulging the melancholy caſt of my own diſpoſition, by painting imaginary diſtreſs; when I recollect not only that theſe were real ſufferings, but that they were ſuſtained by *you!* my mind is overwhelmed with its own ſenſations.—The paper is blotted by my tears—and I can hold my pen no longer.

LETTER

LETTER XVII.

＊"THE moral world,
Which though to us it ſeem perplex'd, moves on
In higher order ; fitted, and impell'd,
By Wiſdom's fineſt hand, and iſſuing all
In univerſal good."

Monſ. and Madame du F——— were
relieved from this extremity of diſtreſs at
a moment ſo critical, and by means ſo
unexpected, that it ſeems the hand of
Heaven viſibly interpoſed in behalf of
oppreſſed virtue. Early in the morning
of that fatal day when they were to leave
their laſt ſad ſhelter, Monſ. du F———
went out, and, in the utmoſt diſtraction of
mind, wandered through ſome of the
ſtreets in the neighbourhood. He was
ſtopped by a gentleman whom he had
known at Geneva, and who told him that

* Thompſon.

he

he was then in fearch of his lodging, having a letter to deliver to him from a Genevois clergyman. Monf. du F—— opened the letter, in which he was informed by his friend, that, fearing he might be involved in difficulties, he had tranfmitted ten guineas to a banker in London, and intreated Monf. du F—— would accept that fmall relief, which was all he could afford, as a teftimony of friendfhip. Monf. du E—— flew to the banker's, received the money as the gift of Heaven, and then, haftening to his wife and child, bade them live a little longer.

A fhort time after, he obtained a fituation as French ufher at a fchool; and Madame du F——, when fhe had a little recovered her ftrength, put out her infant to nurfe, and procured the place of Frence teacher at a boarding-fchool.—— They were now enabled to fupport their child, and to repay the generous affiftance of their kind friend at Geneva. At this period they heard of the death of their fon, whom they left at Caen.

Monf.

Monf. and Madame du F——— paffed
two years in this fituation, when they
were again plunged into the deepeft diftrefs.   A French jeweller was commiffi-
oned by the Baron du F———, to go to his
fon and propofe to him conditions of reconciliation. This man told Monf. du
F——— that his father was juft recovered
from a fevere and dangerous illnefs, and
that his eldeft daughter had lately died.—
Thefe things, he faid, had led him to reflect with fome pain on the feverity he
had exercifed towards his fon ; that the
feelings of a parent were awakened in his
bofom ; and that if Monf. du F———would
throw himfelf at his father's feet, and afk
forgivnefs, he would not fail to obtain it,
and would be allowed a penfion on which
he might live with his wife in England.
In confirmation of thefe affurances, this
man produced feveral letters which he had
received from the Baron to that effect ;
who, as a farther proof of his fincerity,
                                        had

had given this agent seven hundred pounds to put into the hands of Monf. du F—— for the fupport of his wife and child during his abfence. The agent told him, that he had not been able to bring the money to England, but would immediately give him three drafts upon a merchant of reputation in London, with whom he had connections in bufinefs; the firft draft payable in three months, the fecond in fix, and the third in nine.

Monf. du F—— long deliberated upon thefe propofals. He knew too well the vindictive fpirit of his father, not to feel fome dread of putting himfelf into his power. But his agent continued to give him the moft folemn affurances of fafety; and Monf. du F—— thought it was not improbable that his fifter's death might have foftened the mind of his father. He reflected that his marriage had difappointed thofe ambitious hopes of a great alliance, which his father had fondly indulged, aad to whom he owed at leaft,

the

the reparation of haftening to implore his forgivenefs when he was willing to beftow it. What alfo weighed ftrongly on his mind was the confideration that the fum which his father had offered to depofit for the ufe of his wife, would, in cafe any finifter accident fhould befal him, afford a fmall provifion for her and his infant.

The refult of thefe deliberations was, that Monf. du F—— determined (and who can much blame his want of prudence?) he determined to confide in a father!—to truft in that inftinctive affection, which, far from being connected with any peculiar fenfibility of mind, it requires only to be a parent to feel—an affection, which, not confined to the human heart, foftens the ferocioufnefs of the tyger, and fpeaks with a voice that is heard amidft the howlings of the defart. Monf. du F——, after the repeated promifes of his father, almoft confidered that
fufpicion

suspicion which still hung upon his mind as a crime. But least it might be possible that this agent was commissioned to deceive him, he endeavoured to melt him into compassion for his situation. He went to the village where his child was at nurse, and, bringing her six miles in his arms, presented her to this man, telling him, that the fate of that poor infant rested upon his integrity. The man took the innocent creature in his arm, kissed her, and then, returning her to her father, renewed all his former assurances. Monf. du F—— listened and believed. Alas! how difficult is it for a good heart to suspect human nature of crimes which make one blush for the species! How hard is it for a mind glowing with benevolence, to believe that the bosom of another harbours the malignity of a demon!

Monf. du F—— now fixed the time for hs departure with his father's agent, who was to accompany him to Normandy.

dy. Madame du F——— faw the preparations for his journey with anguifh which fhe could ill conceal. But fhe felt that the delicacy of her fituation forbad her interference It was fhe who had made him an alien from his family, and an exile from his country. It was for her, that, renouncing rank, fortune, friends, and connections, all that is efteemed moft valuable in life, he had fuffered the laft extremity of want, and now fubmitted to a ftate of drudgery and dependance. Would he not have a right to reproach her weaknefs, if fhe attempted to oppofe his reconciliation with his father, and exerted that influence which fhe poffeffed over his mind, in order to detain him in a fituation fo remote from his former expectations? She was, therefore, fenfible, that the duty, the gratitude fhe owed her hufband, now required on her part the abfolute facrifice of her own feelings: fhe fuffered without complaint,

complaint, and endeavoured to refign herfelf to the will of Heaven.

The day before his departure, Monf. du F—— went to take leave of his little girl. At this moment a dark and melancholy prefage feemed to agitate his mind. He preffed the child for a long while to his bofom, and bathed it with his tears. The nurfe eagerly enquired what was the matter, and affured him that the child was p rfectly well. Monf. du F—— had no power to reply: he continued clafping his infant in his arms, and at length, tearing himfelf from her in filence, he rufhed out of the houfe.

When the morning of his departure came, Madame du F——, addreffing herfelf to his fellow-traveller, faid to him, with a voice of fupplication, " I entruft you, Sir, with my hufband, with the father of my poor infant, our fole protecter and fupport !—have compaffion on the widow and the orphan !" The man, cafting casting upon her a gloomy look, gave her a cold answer, which made her soul shrink within her.   When Monf. du F—— got into the Brighthelmstone stage, he was unable to bid her farewell; but when the carriage drove off, he put his head out of the window, and continued looking after her, while she fixed her eyes on him, and might have repeated with Imogen.

" I would have broke mine eye-strings;
" Crack'd them, but to look upon him; till the di-
        " minution
" Of space had pointed him sharp as my needle;
" Nay, followed him, till he had melted from
" The smallness of a gnat to air; and then——
" Then turn'd mine eye and wept!"

When the carriage was out of sight, she summoned all her strength, and walked with trembling steps to the school where she lived as a teacher.   With much difficulty she reached the door; but her limbs could support her no longer, and she

fhe fell down fenfelefs at the threfhold.—
She was carrried into the houfe, and reftored to life and the fenfations of mifery.

H   LETTER

LETTER XVIII.

MONS. du F——arrived at his father's chateau in Normandy, in June 1778, and was received by Monf. le Baron, and all his family, with the moft affectionate cordiality. In much exultation of mind, he difpatched a letter to Madame du F——, containing this agreeable intelligence; but his letter was far from producing in her mind the effect he defired. A deep melancholy had feized her thoughts, and her foreboding heart refufed to fympathize in his joy. Short, indeed, was its duration. He had not been many days at the chateau, when he perceived, with furprize and confternation, that his fteps were continually watched by two fervants armed with fufees.

His father now fhewed him an arret, which, on the fourth of June, 1776, he

had

had obtained from the Parliament of Rouen against his marriage.   The Baron then ordered his son to accompany him to his house at Rouen, whither they went, attended by several servants.   That evening, when the attendants withdrew after supper, the Baron, entirely throwing off the mask of civility and kindness, which he had worn in such opposition to his nature, reproached his son in terms of the utmost bitterness, for his past conduct, inveighed against his marriage, and, after having exhausted every expression of rage and resentment, at length suffered him to retire to his own apartment.

There the unhappy Monf. du F——, absorbed in the most gloomy reflections, lamented in vain that fatal credulity which had led him to put himself into the power of his implacable father.   At the hour of midnight his meditations were interrupted by the sound of feet approaching his chamber; and in a few moments the door was thrown open, and his father, at-

H 2   termined

tended by a fervant armed, and two * Cavaliers de Marechauffée, entered the room. Refiftance and fupplication were alike unavailing. Monf. du F——'s papers were feized; a few louis d'ors, which conftituted all the money he poffeffed, were taken from him; and he was conducted in the dead of night, July the 7th, 1778, to St. Yon., a convent ufed as a place of confinement near Rouen, where he was thrown into a dungeon.

A week after his father entered the dungeon. You will perhaps conclude that his hard heart felt at length the relentings of a parent. You will at leaft fuppofe, that his imagination being haunted, and his confcience tormented with the image of a fon ftretched on the floor of this fubterraneous cell, he could fupport the idea no longer, and had haftened to give repofe to his own mind by releafing his captive. Far different were the motives of his vifit. He confidered

* Officers of juftice.

that

that such was his son's attachment to his wife, that, so long as he believed he had left her in possession of seven hundred pounds, he would find comfort from that consideration, even in the depth of his dungeon. His father, therefore, hastened to remove an error from the mind of his son, which left the measure of his woes unfilled. Nor did he chuse to yield to another the office of inflicting a pang sharper than captivity; but himself informed his son, that the merchant, who was to pay the seven hundred pounds to his wife, was declared a bankrupt.

A short time after, the Baron du F—— commenced a suit at law against that agent of iniquity whom he had employed to deceive his son, and who, practising a refinement of treachery of which the Baron was not aware, had kept the seven hundred pounds, with which he was intrusted, and given drafts upon a merchant who he knew would fail before the time of payment. Not being able to pro-

H 3 secute

fecute this affair without a power of at-
torney from his fon, the Baron applied to
him for that purpofe. But Monf. du
F———, being firmly refolved not to deprive his wife of the chance of recovering
the money for herfelf and her child, could
by no intreaties or menaces be led to comply. In vain his father, who had confented to allow him a few books, ordered him to be deprived of that refource,
and that his confinement fhould be rendered ftill more rigorous; he continued
inflexible.

Monf. du F——— remained in his prifon
without meeting with the fmalleft mark of
fympathy from any one of his family tho'
his fecond brother, Monf. de B———, was
now eighteen years of age; an age at
which the fordid confiderations of intereft, how much foever they may affect
our conduct at a more advanced period of
life, can feldom ftifle thofe warm and
generous feelings which feem to belong
to youth. It might have been expected
that

that this young man would have abhorred the prospect of possessing a fortune
which was the just inheritance of his brother, and which could only be obtained
by detaining that brother in perpetual
captivity. Even admitting that his inex-
orable father prohibited his visiting the
prison of his brother, his heart should
have told him, that disobedience, in this
instance, would have been virtue: Or,
was it not sufficient to remain a passive
spectator of injustice, without becoming,
as he afterwards did, the agent of cruelty inflicted on a brother?

Where are the words that can convey
an adequate idea of the sufferings of Madame du F—— during this period?
Three weeks after her husband's departure from England, she heard the general
report of the town of Rouen, that the
Baron du F—— had obtained a letter de
cachet against his son, and thrown him
into prison. This was all she heard of
her husband for the space of two years.

Ignorant

Ignorant of the place of his confinement,
uncertain if he ſtill lived, perhaps her mi-
ſeries were even more poignant than his.
In the diſmal ſolitude of a priſon, his
pains were alleviated by the ſoothing reflection that he ſuffered for her he loved;
while that very idea was to her the moſt
bitter aggravation of diſtreſs. Her days
paſſed in anguiſh, which can only be con-
ceived where it has been felt, and her
nights were diſturbed by the gloomy wan-
derings of fancy. Sometimes ſhe ſaw
him in her dreams chained to the floor of
his dungeon, his boſom bathed in blood,
and his countenance disfigured by death.
Sometimes ſhe ſaw him haſtening towards
her, when at the moment that he was
going to embrace her, they were fiercely
torn a ſunder. Madame du F—— was
naturally of a delicate conſtitution, and
grief of mind reduced her to ſuch a de-
plorable ſtate of weakneſs, that it was
with infinite difficulty ſhe performed the
                                    duties

duties of her situation. For herself, she would have welcomed death with thankfulness; but she considered that her child now depended entirely on her labours for support: and this was a motive sufficiently powerful to prompt her to the careful prefervation of her own life, though it had long become a burden. The child was three years old when her father left England; recollected him perfectly; and, whenever her mother went to visit her, used to call with eagerness for her papa. The enquiry, in the voice of her child, of " When shall I fee my dear, dear papa?" was heard by this unhappy mother with a degree of agony which it were vain indeed to describe.

LETTER

L E T T E R XIX.

Mons. du F——was repeatedly offered his liberty, but upon conditions
which he abhorred. He was required
for ever to renounce his wife; who, while
she remained with her child in a distant
country, was to receive from his father a
small pension, as an equivalent for the
pangs of disappointed affection, of dis-
grace and dishonour.   With the indignation of offended virtue he spurned at these
insulting propositions, and endeavoured
to prepare his mind for the endurance of
perpetual captivity.

Nor can imagination form an idea of a
scene more dreadful than his prison, where
he perceived with horror that the greatest number of those prisoners who had
been many years in confinement, had an

appear-

appearance of frenzy in their looks, which
shewed that reason had been too weak for
the long struggle with calamity, and had
at last yielded to despair. In a cell adjoining Monf. du F——'s, was an old man
who had been confined nearly forty years.
His grey beard hung down to his waist,
and, during the day, he was chained by his
neck to the wall. He was never allowed
to leave his cell, and never spoke; but
Monf. du F—— used to hear the rattling
of his chains.

The prisoners, a few excepted, were
generally brought from their cells at
the hour of noon, and dined together.
But this gloomy repast was served in
uninterrupted silence. They were not
suffered to utter one word, and the pe-
nalty of transgressing this rule was a rigorous confinement of several weeks. As
soon as this comfortless meal was finished,
the prisoners were instantly obliged to
return to their dungeons, in which they
were

were locked up till the same hour the following day. Monf. du F------, in his damp and melancholy cell, paffed two winters without fire, and fuffered fo feverely from cold, that he was obliged to wrap himfelf up in the few clothes which covered his bed. Nor was he allowed any light, except that which during the fhort day beamed through the fmall grated window in the cieling of his dungeon.

Is it not difficult to believe that thefe fufferings were inflicted by a father? A father!—— that name which I cannot trace without emotion; which conveys all the ideas of protection, of fecurity, of tendernefs;—that dear relation to which, in general, children owe their profperity, their enjoyments, and even their virtues!—Alas, the unhappy Monf. du F—— owed nothing to *his* father, but that life, which from its earlieft period his cruelty had embittered, and which

which he now condemned to languifh in miferies that death only could heal.

A young gentleman, who was confined in a cell on one fide of Monf. du F——'s, contrived to make a fmall hole through the wall; and thefe companions in misfortune, by placing themfelves clofe to the hole, could converfe together in whifpers. But the monks were not long in difcovering this, and effectually deprived them of fo great an indulgence, by removing them to diftant cells. Thefe unrelenting Monks, who performed with fuch fidelity their office of tormenting their fellow creatures, who never relaxed in one article of perfecution, and adhered with fcrupulous rigour to the code of cruelty, were called, *" Les Freres de la fainte Charité." One among them deferved the appellation. This good old Monk ufed to vifit the prifoners by ftealth, and endeavour to ad-

* The Brothers of the holy Charity.

minifter

minifter comfort to their affliction. Often he repeated to Monf. du F———, * "Mon cher frere, confolez vous ; mettez votre confiance en Dieu, vos maux feront finis !"

Monf. du F—— remained two years in prifon without receiving any intelligence of his wife, on whofe account he fuffered the moft diftracting anxiety. He had reafon to apprehend that her frame, which had already been enfeebled by her misfortunes, would fink beneath this additional load of mifery, and that fhe would perhaps be rendered unable to procure that little pittance, which might preferve herfelf and her child from want. At length one of his fellow-prifoners, who was going to regain his liberty, took charge of a letter to Madame du F——, and flattered him with the hope of finding

* My dear brother. be comforted ; place your confidence in God, your afflictions will have an end.

fome

some means of transmitting to him an answer.

The letter paints so naturally the situation of his mind, that I have translated some extracts from it.

" My thoughts (he says) are unceas-
" ingly occupied about you, and my
" dear little girl. I am for ever recall-
" ing the blessed moments when I had
" the happiness of being near you, and
" at that recollection my tears refuse to
" be controuled. How could I con-
" sent to separate myself from what was
" most dear to me in the world ? No
" motive less powerful than that of seek-
" ing your welfare, and that of my child,
" could have determined me—and alas!
" I have not accomplished this end. I
" know too well that you have never
" received that sum of money which I
" thought I had secured for you, and for
" which I risked the first blessing of life.
" What fills my mind with the greatest
                                    " horror,

" horror, in the folitude of my prifon, is
" the fear that you are fuffering difficul-
" ties in a foreign country. Here I re-
" main ignorant of your fate, and can
" only offer to Heaven the moft ardent
" vows for your welfare.

" What joy would a letter from you
" give me! but I dare not flatter myfelf
" with the hope of fuch fweet confola-
" tion. All I can affure myfelf of is,
" that though feparated, perhaps for ever,
" our fouls are united by the moft ten-
" der friendfhip and attachment. Per-
" haps I may not find it poffible to
" write to you again for a long while;
" but be affured that no menaces, no fuf-
" ferings, no dungeons fhall ever fhake
" my fidelity to you, and that I fhall love
" you to the laft hour of my exiftence.
" I find a confolation in the reflection that
" it is for you I fuffer. If Providence
" ever permits us to meet again, that
" moment will efface the remembrance
                                    " of

" of all my calamities. Live, my dear-
" eft wife, in that hope. I conjure you
" preferve your life for my fake, and for
" the fake of our dear little girl! Em-
" brace her tenderly for me, and defire
" her alfo to embrace you for her poor
" papa. I need not recommend my
" child to the care of fo tender a mother;
" but I conjure you to infpire her mind
" with the deepeft fenfe of religion. If
" fhe is born to inherit the misfortunes
" of her father, this will be her beft
" fource of confolation.

" Whatever offers may be made you
" by my father, I exhort you never have
" the weaknefs to liften to them, but
" preferve your rights, and thofe of my
" dear little girl, which, perhaps, may
" one day be of fome value. If you are
" ftill at Mrs. D——'s boarding-fchool,
" tell her that I recommend my wife and
" child to her compaffion.—— But-
" what am I faying? I am ignorant if you
are

" are ſtill with her, ignorant whether
" the deareſt objects of my affection ſtill
" live! But I truſt that Providence has
" preſerved you. Adieu! May God
" Almighty bleſs you, and my child! I
" never ceaſe imploring him to have pity
" on the widow and the orphan in a land
" of ſtrangers."

LETTER

LETTER XX.

YOU, my dear friend, who have felt the tender attachments of love and friendfhip, and the painful anxieties which abfence occafions, even amidft fcenes of variety and pleafure; who underftand the value at which tidings from thofe we love is computed in the arithmetic of the heart; who have heard with almoft uncontroulable emotion the poftman's rap at the door; have trembling feen the well-known hand which excited fenfations that almoft deprived you of power to break the feal which feemed the talifman of happinefs: you can judge of the feelings of Monf. Du F—— when he received, by means of the fame friend who had conveyed his letter, an anfwer from his wife. But the perfon who

brought

brought the letter to his dungeon, dreading the rifk of a difcovery, infifted, that after having read it, he fhould return it to him immediately. Monf. du F——— preffed the letter to his heart, bathed it with his tears, and implored the indulgence of keeping it at leaft till the next morning. He was allowed to do fo, and read it till every word was imprinted on his memory; and, after enjoying the fad luxury of holding it that night on his bofom, was forced the next morning to relinquifh his treafure.

On the 10th of October, 1780, the Baron Du F——— came to the convent, and ordered the monks to bring his fon from his dungeon to the parloir, and leave them together. With the utmoft reluctance Monf. du F——— obeyed this fummons, having long loft all hope of foftening the obdurate heart of his father. When the Monks withdrew, the Baron began upbraiding him the moft bitter

terms,

terms, for his obstinate resistance to his will, which, he informed him, had availed nothing, as he had gained his suit at law, and recovered the seven hundred pounds. Monf. du F—— replied, that the pain he felt from his intelligence would have been far more acute, had his wife been deprived, with his concurrence, of the money which was promised for her subsistence, and on the reliance of which promise he had been tempted to leave England. His father then enquired if he still persisted in his adherance to the disgraceful connection he had formed; to which his son answered, that not merely were his affections interested, but that his honour obliged him to maintain, with inviolable fidelity, a solemn and sacred engagement. The rage of the Baron, at these words, became unbounded. He stamped the ground with his feet; he aimed a stroke at his son, who, taking advantage of this moment of frenzy, determined

termined to attempt his efcape ; and, rufh
ing out of the apartment, and avoiding
that fide of the convent which the monks
inhabited, he endeavoured to find his way
to the garden, but miffed the paffage
which led to it. He then flew up a ftair-
cafe, from which he heard the voice of
his father calling for affiftance. Finding
that all the doors which he paffed were
fhut, he continued afcending till he reached the top of the building, where meeting with no other opening than a hole
made in the floping roof to let in light to
a garret, he climbed up with much difficulty, and then putting his feet through
the hole, and letting his body out by de-
grees, he fupported himfelf for a moment
on the roof, and deliberated on what he
was about to do. But his mind was, at
this crifis, wrought up to a pitch of def-
peration, which mocked the fuggeftions
of fear. He quitted his hold, and, fling-
ing himfelf from a height of nearly fifty
feet,

feet, became infenfible before he reached the ground, where he lay weltering in his blood, and to all appearance dead.

He had fallen on the high road leading from Rouen to Caen. Some people who were paffing gathered round him, and one perfon having wafhed the blood from his face, inftantly recognized his features, and exclaimed to the aftonifhed croud, that he was the eldeft fon of the Baron Du F—— Upon examining his body, it was found that he had broken his arm, his thigh, his ancle-bone, and his heel, befides having received many violent bruifes. He ftill remained in a ftate of infenfibility; and, while thefe charitable ftrangers were ufing their efforts to reftore him to life, the monks haftened from their convent, fnatched their victim from thofe good Samaritans who would have poured oil and wine into his wounds, and carried him to the infirmary of the convent, where he remained fome weeks

before

before he recovered his fenfes; after which he lay ftretched upon a bed for three Months, fuffering agonies of pain.

His father, who had been the jailor, and almoft the murderer of his fon, heard of thefe fufferings without remorfe, nor did he ever fee him more. But, though he was fufficiently obdurate to bear unmoved the calamities he had inflicted on his child, though he could check the upbraidings of his own confcience, he could not filence the voice of public indignation. The report that Monf. du F—— had been found lying on the road bathed in blood, and had in that condition been dragged to the prifon of S. Yon, was foon fpread through the town of Rouen. Every one fympathized in the fate of this unfortunate young man, and execrated the tyranny of his unrelenting father.

The univerfal clamour reached the ear of his brother, Monf. De B——, who now, for the firft time, out of refpect to

the

the public opinion, took a measure which
his heart had never dictated during the
long captivity of his brother, that of visiting him in prison. Monf. de B——'s
design in these visits was merely to appease
the public; for small indeed was the consolation they afforded to his brother. He
did not come to bathe with his tears the
bed where that unhappy young man lay
stretched in pain and anguish; to lament
the severity of his father; to offer him
all the consolation of fraternal tenderness:—he came to warn him against indulging a hope of ever regaining his liberty—he came to pierce his soul with
" hard unkindness' altered eye, which
mocks the tear it forc'd to flow!"

I will not attempt to describe the
wretchedness of Madame du F——,
when she heard the report of her hufband's situation. Your heart will con-
ceive what she suffered far better than I
can relate it. Three months after his
fall, Monf. du F—— contrived, through

the

the affiftance of the charitable old monk,
to fend her a few lines written with his
left hand. "My fall " (he fays) "has
" made my captivity known, and has led
" the whole town of Rouen to take an
" intereft in my misfortunes. Perhaps I
" fhall have reafon to blefs the accident,
" which may poffibly prove the means of
" procuring me my liberty, and uniting
" me again to you !—In the mean time,
" I truft that Providence will watch with
" paternal goodnefs over the two objects
" of my moft tender affection. Do not,
" my deareft wife, fuffer the thoughts of
" my fituation to prey too much upon
" your mind. My arm is almoft well :
" my thigh and foot are not quite cured ;
" but I am getting better.

" I could not fupprefs my tears on read-
" ing that part of your letter, wherein you
" tell me that my dear little girl often
" afks for her papa.—Kifs her for me a
" thoufand times, and tell her that her
" papa is always thinking of her and her
,, dear

" dear mama. I am well convinced that
" you will give her the best education
" your little pittance can afford. But
" above all, I beseech you, inspire her
" young mind with sentiments of piety:
" teach her to love her Creator: that is
" the most essential of all lessons. Adieu,
" dearest and most beloved of women!—
" Is there a period in reserve when we
" shall meet again? Oh how amply will
" that moment compensate for all our
" misfortunes!"

LETTER

LETTER XXI.

AT length the Parliament of Rouen began to interest itself in the cause of Monf. du F———. The circumstances of his confinement were mentioned in that Affembly, and the Prefident fent his Secretary to Monf. du F———'s prifon, who had now quitted his bed, and was able to walk with the affiftance of crutches. By the advice of the Prefident, Monf. du F——— addreffed fome letters to the Parliament, reprefenting his fituation in the moft pathetic terms, and imploring their interference in his behalf.

It is here neceffary to mention, that Monf. de Bel B———, Procureur General de Rouen, being intimately connected with the Baron du F———'s family, had ventured to demonftrate his friendfhip for

the

the Baron; by confining his fon nearly
three years on his own authority, and
without any lettre de cachet. And, though
Monf. de Bel B—— well knew, that
every fpecies of oppreffion was connived
at, under the fhelter of lettres de cachet,
he was fenfible that it was only beneath
their aufpices that the exercife of tyranny
was permitted ; and in this particular in-
ftance, not having been cruel * felon les
regles, he apprehended, that if ever Monf.
du F—— regained his liberty, he might
be made refponfible for his conduct. He,
therefore, exerted all his influence, and
with too much fuccefs, to fruftrate the be-
nevolent intention of the Prefident of the
Parliament, refpecting Monf. du F——.
His letters were indeed read in that Affembly, and ordered to be registered
where they ftill remain a record of the pu-
fillanimity of thofe men, who fuffered the

---

* According to rules.

authority

authority of Monf. de Bel B——— to overcome the voice of humanity; who acknowledged the atrocity of the Baron du F——'s conduct, and yet were deaf to the fupplications of his fon, while, from the depth of his dungeon, he called upon them for protection and redrefs.

May the fate of the captive, in the land of France, no more hang fufpended on the frail thread of the pity, or the caprice of individuals! May juftice erect, on eternal foundations, her protecting fanctuary for the oppreffed; and may humanity and mercy be the graceful decorations of her temple!

The Baron du F——— perceived that, notwithftanding his machinations had prevented the Parliament of Rouen from taking any effectual meafures towards liberating his fon, it would be impoffible to filence the murmurs of the public, while he remained confined at St. Yon. He determined, therefore, to remove him

to

to some distant prison, where his name,
and family were unknown; and where,
beyond the jurisdiction of the Parliament
of Rouen, his groans might rise unpitied
and unavenged. But the Baron, not
daring, amidst the general clamour, to remove his son by force, edeavoured to
draw him artfully into the snare he had
prepared.

Monf. de B—— was sent to his brother's prison, where he represented to him,
that, though he must not indulge the least
hope of ever regaining his liberty, yet, if
he would write a letter to Monf. M——,
keeper of the seals, desiring to be removed
to some other place, his confinement should
be made far less rigorous. Monf. du
F—— was now in a state of desperation,
that rendered him almost careless of his
fate. He perceived that the Parliament
had renounced his cause. He saw no possibility to escape from St. Yon; and flattered himself, that in a place where he was
less

lefs clofely confined, it might perhaps be
practicable ; and therefore he confented
to write the letter required, which Monf.
de B—— conveyed in triumph to his
father. There were, however, fome expreffions in the letter which the Baron
difapproved, on which account he returned
it, defiring that thofe expreffions might be
changed. But, during the interval of his
brother's abfence, Monf. du F—— had
reflected on the rafh imprudence of con-
fiding in the promifes of thofe by whom
he had been fo cruelly deceived. No
fooner, therefore, did Monf. de B——
put the letter again into his hands, than
he tore it into pieces, and peremptorily
refufed to write another.

Soon after this, Monf. du B——, the
ambaffador of the tyrant, again returned
to his brother with frefh credentials, and
declared to him, that if he would write
to the keeper of the feals, defiring to be
removed from St. Yon, he fhould, in one
fortnight

fortnight after his removal, be restored to liberty. Upon Monf. du F——'s af-serting that he could no longer confide in the promiſes made him by his family, his brother, in a formal written engagement, to which he ſigned his name, gave him the moſt ſolemn aſſurance, that this pro-miſe ſhould be fulfilled with fidelity. Monf. du F—— deſired a few days for deliberation, and, during that interval, found means of conſulting a magiſtrate of Rouen who was his friend, and who adviſed him to comply with the terms that were offered, after having cauſed ſe-veral copies of the written engagement to be taken, and certified by ſuch of the priſoners at St. Yon as were likely to re-gain their freedom; a precaution necef-ſary, leſt his own copy ſhould be torn from his hands.

Thus, having neither truſted to the af-fection, the mercy, or the remorſe of thoſe within whoſe boſoms ſuch ſentiments were extinguiſhed;

extinguifhed; having bargained, by a written agreement, with a father and a brother, for his releafe from the horrors of perpetual captivity, Monf. du F——— wrote the letter required.

Soon after, an order was fent from Verfailles for his releafe from the prifon of St. Yon, and with it a lettre de cachet, whereby he was exiled to Beauvais, with a command not to leave that town. Monf. de B———, acting as a * Cavalier de la Marechauffée, conducted his brother to this place of exile, and there left him. A fhort time after, Monf. du F——— received an intimation, from that magiftrate of Rouen who had interefted himfelf in his misfortunes, that his father was on the point of obtaining another lettre de cachet, to remove him from Beauvais, to fome prifon in the fouth of France, where he might never more be heard of·

* An officer of juftice.

This

This gentleman added, that Monf. du F—— had not one moment to lofe, and advifed him immediately to attempt his efcape.

Early on the morning after he received this intelligence, Monf. du. F——, who had the liberty to walk about the town, fled from Beauvais. The perfon who brought him the letter from the magiftrate, waited for him at a little diftance from the town, and accompanied him on his journey. When they reached Lifle in Flanders, not having a paffport, they were obliged to wait from eleven o'clock at night till ten the next morning, before they could obtain permiffion from the Governor to proceed on their journey. Monf. du F—— concluded that he was purfued, and fuffered the moft dreadful apprehenfions of being overtaken. His companion, with fome addrefs, at length obtained a paffport, and attended him as far as Oftend. The wind proving contrary

trary, he was detained two days in a state of the most distracting inquietude, and concealed himself on board the vessel in which he had taken his passage for England. At length the wind became favourable; the vessel sailed, and arrived late in the night at Margate. Monf. du F——, when he reached the English shore, knelt down, and, in a transport of joy, kissed the earth of that dear country which had twice proved his asylum.

He then enquired when the stage-coach set off for London, and was told that it went at so early an hour the next morning that he could not go till the day after, as he must wait till his portmanteau was examined by the custom-house officers, who were now in bed. The delay of a few hours in seeing his wife and child, after such an absence, after such sufferings, was not to be endured. In a violent agitation of mind, he snatched up his portmanteau, and was going to fling it into

into the fea, when he was prevented by
the people near him, who faid, that if he
would pay the fees, his portmanteau
fhould be fent after him. He eagerly
complied with their demands, and fet out
for London. As he drew near, his anxiety, his impatience, his emotion increafed.
His prefent fituation appeared to him like
one of thofe delicious dreams, which
fometimes vifited the darknefs of his dungeon, and for a while reftored him, in
imagination, to thofe he loved. Scarcely
could he perfuade himfelf that he was
beyond the reach of oppreffion; that he
was in a land of freedom; that he was
haftening every moment towards his wife
and child. When he entered London,
his fenfations became almoft too ftrong to
bear. He was in the very fame place
which his wife and child inhabited—but
were they yet alive? were they in health?
had Heaven indeed referved for him the
tranfport of holding them once more to
his

his bosom, of mixing his tears with theirs? When he knocked at the door of the house where he expected to hear of Madame du F——, he had scarcely power to articulate his enquiries after her and his child. He was told that they were in health, but that Madame du F——, being in a situation six miles from London, he could not see her till the next morning. Mons. du F—— had not been in a bed for several nights, and was almost overcome with agitation and fatigue. He, however, instantly set out on foot for the habitation of his wife, announced himself to the mistress of the family, and remained in another apartment, while she, after making Madame du F—— promise that she would listen to her with calmness, told her, that there was a probability of her husband's return to England He heard the sobs, the exclamations, of his wife at this intelligence—he could restrain no longer—he rushed into the room—he

flew

flew into her arms—he continued pref
fing her in filence to his bofom. She
was unable to fhed a tear; and it was
not till after he had long endeavoured to
footh her by his tendernefs, and had talked
to her of her child, that fhe obtained relief from weeping. She then, with the
moft violent emotion, again and again repeated the fame enquiries, and was a confiderable time before fhe recovered any
degree of compofure.

All the fortune Monf. du F—— poffeffed when he reached London, was one
half guinea; but his wife had, during his
abfence, faved ten guineas out of her little falary You will eafily imagine how
valuable this hoard became in her eftima-
tion, when fhe could apply it to the precious ufe of relieving the neceffities of her
hufband. Monf Du F—— went to
London the next day, and hired a little
garret: there, with a few books, a rufh-
light, and fome ftraw in which he wrap-

ped

ped his legs to supply the want of fire, he recollected not the splendour to which he had once been accustomed, but the dungeon from which he had escaped. He saw his wife and child once a week; and, in those solitary moments, when books failed to sooth his thoughts, he anticipated the hour in which he should again meet the objects most dear to his heart, and passed the intervals of time in philosophic resignation. His clothes being too shabby to admit of his appearing in the day, he issued from his little shed when it was dark, and endeavoured to warm himself by the exercise of walking.

Unfortunately he caught the small-pox, and his disorder rose to such a height, that his life was despaired of. In his delirium, he used to recapitulate the sad story of his misfortunes; and when he saw any person near his bed-side, would call out, with the utmost vehemence, * " Qu'on

* Make all the French go out.

fasse

fafle fortir tous les François!" After
having been for fome days in the moft
imminent danger, Monf. du F—— recovered from this difeafe.

LETTER

LETTER XXII.

SIX months after Monf. du F——'s
return to England, his family found themfelves compelled to filence the public clamours, by allowing him a fmall annual
penfion. Upon this, Madame du F——
quitted her place, and came to live with
her hufband and her child in an obfcure
lodging. Their little income received
fome addition by means of teaching the
French language in a few private families.

A young lady, who came to pay me a
vifit at London in 1785, defired to take
fome leffons in French, and Madame du
F—— was recommended to us for that
purpofe. We foon perceived in her converfation every mark of a cultivated mind,
and of an amiable difpofition. She at
length told us the hiftory of her misfortunes,

tunes, with the pathetic eloquence of her own charming language; and, after having heard that recital, it required but common humanity, to treat her with the respect due to the unhappy, and to feel for her sorrows that sympathy to which they had such claim. How much has the sensibility of Monf. and Madame du F—— over-rated those proofs of esteem, and friendship which we were enabled to shew them in their adversity!—But I must not anticipate.

On the seventh of October, 1787, the Baron died, leaving, besides Monf. du F——, two other fons, and a daughter.

I must here mention, that at the time when Monf. du F—— was confined to his bed in the prifon of St. Yon, from the confequences of his fall, his father, in order to avoid the clamours at Rouen, went for fome weeks to Paris. He there made a will, difinhereting his eldeft fon. By the old laws of France, however, a father could not punifh his fon more than

once

once for the fame offence. Nor was there
any thing in fo mild a claufe that cou'd
much encourage difobedience; fince this
fingle punifhment, of which the mercy
of the law was careful to avoid repetition,
might be extended to refidence for life in
a dungeon. Such was evidently the intention of the Baron du F——: and,
though his fon, difappointing this intention, had efcaped with only three years of
captivity, and fome broken limbs, the be-
nignant law above-mentioned interpofed
to prevent farther punifhment, and left
the Baron without any legal right to deprive Monf. du F—— of his inheritance.
His brothers, being fenfible of this, wrote
to inform him of his father's death, and re-
cal him to France. He refufed to go
while the lettre de cachet remained in
force againft him. The Baron having left
all his papers fealed up, which his younger fons could not open but in the pre-
fence of their brother, they obtained the
revocation of the lettre de cachet, and
fent

fent it to Monf. du F———, who immediately fet off for France.

The Baron's eftate amounted to about four thoufand pounds a year. Willing to avoid a tedious litigation with his brothers, Monf. du F——- confented to divide with them this property. But he foon found reafon to repent of his imprudent generofity; thofe very brothers, on whom he had beftowed an equal fhare of his fortune, refufing to concur with him in his application to the parliament of Rouen for the revocation of the arret againft his marriage. Monf. du F——-, furprifed and fhocked at their refufal, began to entertain fome apprehenfions of his perfonal fafety; and dreading that, fupported by the authority of his mother, another lettre de cachet might be obtained againft him, he haftened back to England. Nor was it till after he had received affurances from feveral of the magiftrates of Rouen, that they would be refponfible for the fafety of his perfon, that

that he again ventured to return to France, accompanied by Madame and Mademoifelle du F——, in order to obtain the revocation of the arret. On their arrival at Rouen, finding that the parliament was exiled, and that the bufinefs could not be profecuted at that time, they again came back to pafs the winter in England.

At this period his mother died; and in the following fummer Monf. and Madame du F—— arrived in France, at the great epocha of French liberty, on the 15th of July, 1789, the very day after that on which the Baftille was taken. It was then that Monf. du F—— felt himfelf in fecurity on his native fhore.—It was then that his domeftic comforts were no longer embittered with the dread of being torn from his family by a feparation more terrible than death itfelf.—It was then that he no more feared that his repofe at night would be broken by the entrance of ruffians prepared to drag him to dungeons,

the

the darkness of which was never visited by the blessed beams of day!

He immediately took possession of his chateau, and only waits for the appointment of the new judges, to solicit the revocation of the arret against his marriage, and to secure the inheritance of his estate to Mademoiselle du F——, his only daughter, who is now fifteen years of age, and is that very child who was born in the bosom of adversity, and whose infancy was exposed to all the miseries of want. May she never know the afflictions of her parents, but may she inherit their virtues!

Under the antient government of France, there might have been some doubt of Monf. du F——'s obtaining the revocation of the arret against his marriage. Beneath the iron hand of despotism, justice and virtue might have been overthrown. But happier omens belong to the new constitution of France. The judges will commence their high office with

with that dignity becoming fo important a truft, by cancelling an act of the moft flagrant oppreffion. They will confirm that folemn, that facred engagement which Monf. and Madame du F—— have three times vowed at the altar of God!— which has been fanctioned by laws human and divine—which has been ratified in earth and in heaven!

No fooner had Monf. and Madame du F------ taken poffeffion of their property, than they feemed eager to convince us, how little this change of fortune was capable of obliterating, for one moment, the remembrance of the friends of their adverfity. With all the earneftnefs of affection they invited us to France, and appeared to think their profperity incomplete, and their happinefs imperfect, till we accepted the invitation. You will believe that we are not infenfible witneffes of the delightful change in their fortune. We have the joy of feeing them, not only poffeffing all the comforts of affluence

fluence, but univerfal refpect and efteem.

Monf. du F——: endeavours to banifh mifery from his poffeffions. His tenants confider him as a father, and, " when the eye fees him it bleffes him." I faid to one of the peafants whom I met in my walk yefterday, * " Je fuis charmée de voir que Monf. eft fi bien aimé ici." —" Oh pour ça, oui Madame, et à bonne raifon, car il ne nous fait que du bien!"

Such is the hiftory of Monf. du F——, Has it not the air of a romance? and are you not glad that the denouement is happy?---Does not the old Baron die exactly in the right place; at the very page one would chufe?---Or, if I fometimes wifh that he had lived a little longer, it is only from that defire of retribution, which, in cafes of injuftice and oppreffion, it is fo natural to feel.----It is only becaufe the knowledge of the overthrow of the an,

* I am happy to fee that Monfieur is fo much beloved.—Oh, yes, Madam; and well he may, he does us nothing but good.

tient

K

tient government would have been a fufficient punifhment to him for all his cruelty. He would have fickened at the
fight of general happinefs. The idea of
liberty being extended to the lower ranks,
while, at the fame time, tyranny was deprived of its privileges, he would have
found infupportable; and would have abhorred a country, which could no longer
boaft of a Baftille; a country where iron
cages were broken down, where dungeons
were thrown open; and where juftice was
henceforth to fhed a clear and fteady light,
without one dark fhade of relief from lettres de cachet.

But peace be to his afhes! If the recollection of his evil deeds excites my indignation, it is far otherwife with Monf.
and Madame du F——. Never did I
hear their lips utter an expreffion of refentment, or difrefpect, towards his memory; and never did I, with that warmth
which belongs to my friendfhip for them,
                              involuntarily

involuntarily paſs a cenſure on his conduct, without being made ſenſible, by
their behaviour, that I had done wrong.

Adieu!

K 2 LETTER

LETTER XXIII.

I Am glad you think that a friend's having been perfecuted, imprifoned, mai-
med, and almoft murdered under the antient government of France, is a good
excufe for loving the revolution. What,
indeed, but friendfhip, could have led my
attention from the annals of imagination
to the records of politics; from the poetry to the profe of human life? In vain
might Ariftocrates have explained to me
the rights of kings, and Democrates have
defcanted on the rights of the people.
How many fine-fpun threads of reafoning
would my wandering thoughts have broken; and how difficult fhould I have
found it to arrange arguments and infe-
rences in the cells of my brain! But
however dull the faculties of my head,
I can

I can affure you, that when a propofition is addreffed to my heart, I have fome quicknefs of perception. I can then decide, in one moment, points upon which philofophers and legiflators have differed in all ages: nor could I be more convinced of the truth of any demonftration in Euclid, than I am, that, that fyftem of politics muft be the beft, by which thofe I love are made happy.

Monf. du F——'s chateau is near the little town of Forges, celebrated for its mineral waters, and much reforted to in fummer on that account. We went to the fountain on pretence of drinking the waters, but in reality to fee the company. The firft morning we made our appearance, the ladies prefented us with nofegays of fine fpreading purple heath, which they called * Bouquets à la fontaine.

* Nofegays of the fountain.

I was

I was told, before I left England, that I should find that French liberty had destroyed French urbanity. But every thing I have seen and heard, since my arrival in France, has contradicted this assertion, and led me to believe that the French will carefully preserve, from the wreck of their monarchical government, the old charter they have so long held of superiority in politeness. I am persuaded the most determined Democrates of the nation, whatever other privileges they may chuse to exercise, will always suffer the privilege of being rude to lie dormant.

In every country it is social pleasure that sheds the most delicious flowers which grow on the path of life; but in France she covers the whole way with roses, and the traveller can scarcely mark its ruggedness. Happy are a people, so fond of talking as the French, in possessing a language modelled to all the charming purposes of conversation. Their turn of expression is a dress that hangs so gracefully

on

on gay ideas, that you are apt to fuppofe
that wit, a quality parfimonioufly diftri-
buted in other countries, is in France as
common as the gift of fpeech. Perhaps
that brilliant phrafeology, which dazzles
a foreigner, may be familiar and common
to a French ear: but how much ingenuity
muft we allow to a people, who have
formed a language, of which the common-
place phrafes give you the idea of wit!

You, who are a reader of Madame Brulart's works, will know, that I am here
on a fort of claffic ground. The Abbaye
de Bobec is but a few miles diftant from
this chateau, and I walk every day in the
foreft where Michel and Jaqueline erected their little hut; which you may remember, having unfortunately built too
low to admit of their ftanding upright,
they comforted themfelves with the reflection, * " Qu'on ne peut pas penfer à
tout:" and, when they were once feat-

* One cannot think of every thing

ed

ed in their dwelling, in which it was a vain attempt to ftand, expatiated on the comforts of being * " chez foi."   Upon enquiry, I have heard that poor Jaque-line, three years after the happy change in her fortune, was killed by a ftroke of lightning, and that Michel (as he was bound to do, being the hero of a ro-mance) died of grief.

The Abbé de Bobec has much reputa-tion in this part of the country for wif-dom ; but a French gentleman, who din-ed with him yefterday, told me this morn-ing, † " Il m'a donné une indigeftion de bon fens."   This is fomething in the ftyle of a young Frenchman, who went to vi-fit an acquaintance of his at Rotterdam, and has ever fince called that worthy gen-tleman, ‡ " La raifon continue (comme

---

* At home.

† He gave me an indigeftion of good fenfe.

‡ Reafoning continued, as you would fpeak of a fever with frefh paroxyfms.

dit la fievre continue) avec des redouble-
mens."

An alarm has been spread, but without any foundation, that the Auſtrian
troops were marching to invade France.
It puts me in mind of the old trick of
the Roman patricians, who, whenever
the plebeians grew refractory, called out,
that the Equi and the Volſci were coming: the Equi and the Volſci, however,
never came.

LETTER

L E T T E R XXIV.

WE have had a fête at the chateau, on the day of St. Auguſtin, who is Monſ. du F------'s patron ; and, though Monſ. is become a proteſtant, I hope he will always ſhow this mark of reſpect to his old friend St. Auguſtin. Indeed I am perfuaded that Luther and calvin, if they had been of our party, would have reconciled their minds to theſe charming rites of ſuperſtition.

The ceremonies began with a diſcharge of fuſées, after which Mademoiſelle du F------ entered the ſaloon, where a great croud were aſſembled, with a crown of flowers in her hand, and addreſſed her father in theſe words:---*"Mon tres cher
"papa,

* " My dearest papa, can I chuſe a more favour-
" able moment to wiſh you an agreeable fête than
" this.

" papa, pourrois-je profiter d'un moment
" plus favorable pour vous souhaiter une
" bonne féte, que celui ou nos bons, et
" *vrais amis* font ici raffemblés, et s'unif-
" fent a moi pour celebrer cet heureux
" jour ? C'eft dans vos biens cher papa,
" c'eft dans votre chateau que la Divine
" Providence nous réunit, pour chanter
" vos vertus, et ce courage héroique qui
" vous a fait fupporter tous vos *Malheurs.*
" L'orage eft paffé, jouiffez maintenant

" this, when our beft, our faithful friends are here
" affembled, and join with me in celebrating this
" happy day ? It is in the midft of your poffeffions,
" my dear papa, it is in your chateau, that Divine
" Providence has re-united us, to declare your virtues,
" tues, and the heroic fortitude with which you have
" fupported your misfortunes. The ftorm is paft,
" and you can now, my dear papa, enjoy the happi-
" nefs you fo well deferve, and the efteem of every
" amiable mind. May your child contribute to your
" felicity ! May the Supreme Being hear the prayers
" which I addrefs to him for the prefervation of a
" tender father, to whom I offer my duty, my grati-
" tude, and the beft affections of my heart !"

" cher

" cher papa du bonheur que vous meri-
" tez fi bien-de l'eftime que vous vous
" étes acquis dans tous les cœurs fenfibles.
" Que votre chere enfant contribue a vo-
" tre felicité, que l'Eternel daigne exau-
" cer les vœux que je lui adreffe pour la
" confervation et le bonheur d'un ten-
" dre pere, a qui j'offre mes homages,
" ma reconnoiffance, et les fentimens
" d'un cœur qui vous eft tout devoué."

She then placed the crown of flowers upon his head, and he embraced her tenderly. A number of ladies advanced, prefented him with nofegays, and were embraced in their turn.

We had feen, while we were at Paris, a charming little piece performed at the Theatre de Monfieur, called, "La Federation, ou La Famille Patriotique," Madame du F------ fent for a copy of this piece, and it was now performed by the company affembled at the chateau. The tenants, with their wives and daughters,

formed

formed the moſt conſiderable part of the audience, and I believe no play, in antient or modern times, was ever acted with more applauſe. My ſiſter took a part in the performance, which I declined doing, till I recollected that one of the principal characters was a ſtatue; upon which, I conſented to perform * le beau role de la ſtatue. And, in the laſt ſcene, I, being the repreſentative of Liberty, appeared with all her uſual attributes, and guarding the conſecrated banners of the nation, which were placed on an altar, on which was inſcribed, in tranſparent letters, † "A la Liberté, 14 Juillet, 1789." One of the performers pointing to the ſtatue, ſays, ‡ "Chaque peuple à décoré cet-

* The fine part of the ſtatue.
† To Liberty, July 14th, 1789.
‡ Every nation has decorated this idol with ſome peculiar attributes.—This cap has been long one of her moſt eloquent emblems.—Can we not add ſome others, which may, perhaps, become no leſs celebrated ?

te

te idole de quelques attributs qui lui font particuliers.---Ce bonnet fur-tout eft devenu un embléme éloquent.--- Ne pourrions-nous pas en ajouter d'autres qui deviendront peut-étres auffi célebres?" He then unfolds a fcarf of national ribband, which had been placed at the foot of the altar, and adds, * "Cette noble echarpe!---Ces couleurs fi bien afforties ne font-elles pas dignes de figurer auffi parmi les attributs de la Liberté?" The fcarf was thrown over my fhoulder, and the piece concluded with † Le Carillon National: after a grand chorus of ‡ *ça ira*, the performers ranged themfelves in order, and *ça ira* was danced. *Ca ira* hung on every lip, *ça ira* glowed on every countenance! Thus do the French, left they fhould be

* That noble fcarf!—are not its aufpicious colours worthy of appearing amongft the attributes of Liberty?
† The national bells.
‡ It will go on.

tempted,

tempted, by pleafure, to forget one moment the caufe of liberty, bind it to their remembrance in the hour of feftivity, with fillets and fcarfs of national ribband; connect it with the found of the viol and the harp, and appoint it not merely to regulate the great movements of government, but to mold the figure of the dance. When the cotillon was finifhed, fome beautiful fire-works were played off, and we then went to fupper. * "Vous êtes bien placée Monf." faid Madame du F——— to a young Frenchman, who was feated between my fifter and me at table. †"Madame," anfwered he, in a ftile truly French, "me voila heureux pour la premiere fois, a vingt trois ans.

After fupper we returned to the faloon, where the gentlemen danced with the

---

* You are well placed, Sir.

† I am made happy, Madam, for the firft time, at three and twenty years of age.

peafant

peafant girls, and the ladies with the peafants.   A more joyous fcene, or a fet of
happier countenances, my eyes never beheld.   When I recollected the former fituation of my friends, the fpectacle before
me feemed an enchanting vifion: I could
not forbear, the whole evening, com-
paring the paft with the prefent, and,
while I meant to be exceedingly merry,
I felt that tears, which would not be fup-
preffed, were gufhing from my eyes---
but they were tears of luxury.

LETTER

LETTER XXV.

A Decree has paffed in the National Affembly, inftituting rewards for literary merit. The propofal met with great oppofition from one of the members, I do not wifh to remember his name, who faid the ftate ftood in need of hufbandmen, not poets; as if the ftate would be encumbered by having both. This gentleman thinks, that, provided wheat and oats flourifh, the culture of *mind* may be difpenfed with; and that, if the fpade and harrow are fharpened, the quill of genius may be ftripped of all its feathers. * Mais, vive l'Affemblée Nationale !... they have determined never to abolifh the *nobility* of the mufes, or deprive the fine arts † *de leurs droits honorifiques.*

* Long live the National Affembly.
† Of their honorary rights.

Apropos

Apropos of poets.---The French have
conquered many old prejudices, but their
prejudice againſt Shakeſpeare ſtill exiſts.
They well know, that though in England
it is our policy, or our pleaſure, to have
an oppoſition on every other ſubject, we
have not one diſſenting voice about
Shakeſpeare; and therefore they allow
that he may, perhaps, deſerve to be the
idol of the Britiſh nation, a ſort of houſe-
hold god whom we delight to honour;
but they have gods of their own to whom
they pay homage, and have little idea that
Shakeſpeare was not only the glory of
England, but of human nature. It would
be a hopeleſs attempt to convince them,
that the genius of their boaſted Corneille
has ſomething of the proud and affected
greatneſs of Lewis the Fourteenth, while
that of Shakeſpeare has more affinity to
the noble dignified ſimplicity of Henry
the Fourth. They repeat, till you are
weary of the remark, that French trage-
dies

dies are regular dramas, while Shake-
fpeare's plays are monftrous. This reminds me of Boileau's anfwer to an author who had brought him a play to read,
of which Boileau difapproved. Sir, exclaimed the enraged author, I defy malice
to fay that my piece tranfgreffes any one
of the rules. " Why, Sir," replied Boileau, " it tranfgreffes the firft rule of all,
that of keeping the reader awake."

The young gentleman who, as I mentioned to you, was confined at St. Yon,
in the cell adjoining Monf. du F-----'s,
and with whom he ufed to converfe in
whifpers through a hole in the wall, is
come to pay a vifit at the chateau. This
young man went very early into the army : but, at the age of twenty, his father
being at St. Domingo, and his mother
confidering her fon as a fpy upon her
conduct, which was fuch as fhrunk from
infpection, obtained a lettre de cachet
againft him, and he was confined three

years

years at St. Yon. He has told me, that, after the firft year, he loft all hope of ever regaining his liberty. A morbid melancholy feized his mind; he lay ftretched on the fame bed for two years; and fometimes refufed to tafte food for feveral days together. When his father, at his return from St. Domingo, came to liberate him, he was fo feeble that he was unable to walk.

His father again left France, and the brother of this young man has fuffered a fate even more fevere than himfelf. At the age of fifteen, he was guilty of fome indifcretions, which incurred the refentment of his unrelenting mother, and another lettre de cachet was obtained.--- " Is there any caufe in nature that makes thefe hard hearts ?"---He was confined ten years, and only releafed when all the prifons were thrown open, by order of the National Affembly. But for this unhappy young man their mercy came too late---

late—His reason was gone for ever! and he was led out of his prison, at the age of five and twenty, a maniac. When the sensibility with which his brother relates these family misfortunes melts us into tears, we are told, * que la tristesse, est la maladie du charbon Anglois, and, will never be tolerated in France.

You will not be surprized to hear that Monf. du F—— has, with great complacency, relinquished his title; and that, being a ci-devant *captive*, as well as a ci-devant *Baron*, he feels that the enjoyment of personal security, the sweetness of domestic comfort, in short, that the common rights of man are of more value than he ever found the rights of nobility in the solitude of his dungeon. He is ready to acknowledge, that confinement in a subterraneous cell, a fall from a height of fifty feet, and the fracture of his limbs,

* Melancholy is the disease of English coal fires.

are

are things which even the title of Baron
çan fcarcely counterbalance; and he therefore drinks a libation, every day after dinner, * à la fanté de l'Affemblée National-
ale, though they have deprived him of
the foothing epithet of Mon-Seigneur.
We, however, fhall foon ceafe to pledge
him in this toaft.   The day of our departure draws near.   We muft leave the
charming fociety at the chateau—we muft
leave the peafants dance under the fhade
of the old elms, while the fetting fun
pours ftreams of liquid gold through the
foliage—we muft leave † Le maitre de
violon, qui fe ride en riant, avec fa mal-
heureufe figure.—All this muft we leave!
—To-morrow is the laft day of our refidence at the chateau.   What a defolate
word is that monofyllable of *laft*—how

* To the health of the National Affembly.

† The player on the violin, who, with his mife-
rable figure, has become wrinkled from laughing.

fad,

fad, how emphatical its meaning!—
There is fomething in it which gives the
moft indifferent things an intereft in our
affections.—I am fure I could write a vo-
lume with this little word for my text;
but I may as well explain myfelf in one
line—I am forry to leave France!

LETTER

L E T T E R XXVI.

London.

WE left France early in September, that we might avoid the equinoctial gales; but were fo unfortunate as to meet, in our paffage from Dieppe to Brighton, with a very violent ftorm. We were two days and two nights at fea, and beat four and twenty hours off the coaft of Brighton; and it would be difficult for you, who have formed your calculations of time on dry land, to guefs what is the length of four and twenty hours in a ftorm at fea. At laft, with great difficulty, we landed on the beach, where we found feveral of our friends and acquaintance, who, fuppofing that we might be among the paffengers, fympathifed with our danger, and were anxious for our prefervation.

Before the ftorm became fo ferious as to exclude every idea but that of preparing

ing to die with compofure, I could not help being diverted with the comments on French cuftoms, and French politics, which paffed in the cabin. " Ah," fays, one man to his companion, " one had need to go to France, to know how to like old England when one gets back again."—" For my part," rejoined ano-. ther, " I've never been able to get drunk once the whole time I was in France--- not a drop of porter to be had---and as for their victuals, they call a bit of meat of a pound and a half, a fine piece of roaft beef."---"And pray," added he, turning to one of the failors, " What do you think of their National Affembly?"-- " Why," fays the failor, " if I ben't mif- taken, the National Affembly has got fome points of from the wind "

I own it has furprized me not a little, fince I came to London, to find that moft of my acquaintance are of the fame opi-

L   nion

nion with the failor.   Every vifitor brings
me intelligence from France full of dif-
may and horror.   I hear of nothing but
crimes, affaffinations, torture, and death.
I am told that every day witneffes a con-
fpiracy; that every town is the fcene of
a maffacred; that every ftreet is blackened
with a gallows, and every highway delug-
ed with blood   I hear thefe things, and
repeat to myfelf, Is this the picture of
France ? Are thefe the images of that univerfal joy, which called tears into my eyes,
and made my heart throb with fympathy?---To me, the land which thefe
mighty magicians have fuddenly covered
with darknefs, where, waving their evil
wand, they have reared the difmal fcaffold,
have clotted the knife of the affaffin with
gore, have called forth the fhriek of def-
pair, and the agony of torture; to me,
this land of defolation appeared dreft in
additional beauty beneath the genial fmile
of liberty.   The woods feemed to caft a

more

more refrefhing fhade and the lawns to wear a brighter verdure, while ths carols of freedom burft from the cottage-of the peafant, and the voice of joy refounded on the hill, and in the valley.

Muft I be told that my mind is perverted, that I am become dead to all fenfations of fympathy, becaufe I do not weep with thofe who have loft a part of their fuperfluities, rather than rejoice that the oppreffed are protected, that the wronged are redreffed, that the captive is fet at liberty, and that the poor have bread? Did the univerfal parent of the human race, implant the feelings of pity in the heart, that they fhould be confined to the artificial wants of vanity, the ideal deprivations of greatnefs ; that they fhould be fixed beneath the dome of the palace, or locked within the gate of the chateau ; without extending one commiferating figh to the wretched hamlet, as if its famifhed inhabitants, though not ennobled by *man*, did not bear, at leaft, the enfigns of nobility ftamped on our nature by God?

Muft I hear the charming focieties, in which I found all the elegant graces of the moft polifhed manners, all the amiable urbanity of liberal and cultivated minds, compared with the moft rude, ferocious, and barbarous levellers that ever exifted? Really, fome of my Englifh acquaintance, whatever objections they may have to republican principles, do, in their difcuffions of French politics, adopt a moft free and republican ftyle of cenfure. Nothing can be more democratical than their mode of expreffion, or difplay a more levelling fpirit, than their unqualified contempt of *all* the leaders of the revolution.

It is not my intention to fhiver lances, in every fociety I enter, in the caufe of the National Affembly. Yet I cannot help remarking, that, fince that Affembly does not prefume to fet it felf up as an example to this country, we feem to have very little right to be furioufly angry, becaufe they think proper to try another fyftem of government themfelves. Why fhould they not be fuffered to make an experiment in politics? I have always been told, that the improvement of every fcience depends upon experiment. But I now hear that, inftead of their new attempt to form the great machine of fociety upon a fimple principle of general amity, upon the FEDERATION of its members, they ought to have repaired the feudal wheels and fprings, by which their anceftors directed its movements. Yet if mankind had always obferved this retrograde motion, it would furely have led them to few acquifitions in virtue, or in knowledge; and we might even have been worfhipping the idols of paganifm at this moment. To forbid, under the pains and penalties of reproach, all attempts of the human mind to advance to

greater

greater perfection, feems to be profcrib-
ing every art and fcience.   And we cannot much wonder that the French, having received fo fmall a legacy of public
happinefs from their forefathers, and being fenfible of the poverty of their own
patrimony, fhould try new methods of
tranfmitting a richer inheritance to their
pofterity.

Perhaps the improvements which mankind may be capable of making in the
art of politics, may have fome refem-
blance to thofe they have made in the art
of navigation.   Perhaps   our   political
plans may hitherto have been fomewhat
like thofe ill-conftructed mifhapen vef-
fels, which, unfit to combat with the
winds and waves, were only ufed by the
antients to convey the warriors of one
country to defpoil and ravage another
neighbouring ftate; which only ferved to
produce an intercourfe of hoftility, a com-
munication of injury, an exchange of ra-
pine

pine and devastation.---But it may possibly be within the compass of human ability to form a system of politics, which, like a modern ship of discovery, built upon principles that defy the opposition of the tempestuous elements (" and passions are the elements of life"---) instead of yielding to their fury makes them observient to its purpose, and sailing sublimely over the untracked ocean, unites those together whom nature seemed for ever to have separated, and throws a line of connection across the divided world.

One cause of the general dislike in which the French revolution is held in this country, is the exaggerated stories which are carefully circulated by such of the aristocrates as have taken refuge in England. They are not all, however, persons of this description. There is now a young gentleman in London, nephew to the Bishop de Sens, who has lost his fortune, his rank, all his high expectations

tions, and yet who has the generosity to applaud the revolution, and the magnanimity to reconcile himself to personal calamities, from the consideration of general good; and who is " faithful found" to his country, " among the faithless," I hope this amiable young Frenchman will live to witness, and to share the honours, the prosperity of that regenerated country: and I also hope that the National Assembly of France will answer the objections of its adversaries in the manner most becoming its own dignity, by forming such a constitution as will render the French nation virtuous, flourishing, and happy.

F I N I S.

Lightning Source UK Ltd.
Milton Keynes UK
UKOW07f2337280916

284077UK00008B/359/P

9 781140 664758